Henry Harris Jessup

The Setting of the Crescent and the Rising of the Cross

Kamil Abdul Messiah, A Syrian Convert from Islam to Christianity

Henry Harris Jessup

The Setting of the Crescent and the Rising of the Cross
Kamil Abdul Messiah, A Syrian Convert from Islam to Christianity

ISBN/EAN: 9783744727587

Printed in Europe, USA, Canada, Australia, Japan

Cover: Foto ©Lupo / pixelio.de

More available books at **www.hansebooks.com**

The Setting of the Crescent and the Rising of the Cross

KAMIL

ABDUL MESSIAH

A Syrian Convert from Islam to Christianity

BY

THE REV. HENRY HARRIS JESSUP, D.D.
For Forty-one Years a Missionary in Syria

PHILADELPHIA
THE WESTMINSTER PRESS
1898

KAMIL ABDUL MESSIAH.

AUTHOR'S PREFACE.

This book has been written as a labor of love. Its subject was one of nature's noblemen.

It is not easy for a Mohammedan to embrace Christianity, but Kamil's history shows that when he is converted the Moslem becomes a strong and vigorous Christian. The element of divine truth which Mohammed derived from the Old and New Testaments, and which runs like a vein of gold through that extraordinary book, the Koran, teaching the existence and attributes of God, the responsibility of man, and a final judgment, is a good foundation to build upon.

But to reach the foundation; to sweep away the rubbish of childish fables, traditions, and perversions which overlie the original monotheism of the Old Testament, and disarm the accumulated prejudices of twelve centuries—this is the work of the divine Spirit.

Kamil was plainly taught by the Spirit, who revealed Christ to him as his personal Saviour. May it prove to be true that he was but the first-fruits of a mighty harvest to be gathered for Christ among the Mohammedans of the Arab race!

HENRY H. JESSUP.

BEIRUT, SYRIA, *October, 1897.*

INTRODUCTION.

The simple story of the brief Christian life of Kamil Aietany, written by Rev. Dr. Jessup, furnishes a striking illustration of the power of the gospel over the human heart, even when intrenched in the most inveterate types of error.

A young Moslem visits the Jesuit school in Beirut for the special purpose of studying the Greek language. He there gains some partial views of the truth of the New Testament which had previously been withheld from him. He secures a Bible, but this is taken from him by his father. He is then advised by his Jesuit instructors to secure another, and to disarm his father's prejudices by telling him that he desires to learn Christian doctrines only that he may know how to overthrow them in the interest of Islam. At this dishonest suggestion his whole moral nature revolts and he repairs to the study of Dr. Jessup.

At this point a new history began. Not daring to take a Bible home with him, he resorted to the missionary's study day after day and there drank deeply of the precious truth. His heart was evidently moved by the Holy Spirit. Repairing, at length, to the training school under the direction of Rev. Mr. Hardin, in the Lebanon village of Suk-el-Gharb, he found others who were in sympathy with him. Among them was a young Bedawi from the interior who was equally anxious to learn the truth and who also gave evidence of sincere belief in the gospel. What was more important to Kamil's future was his acquaintance with Rev. Mr. Cantine of the Reformed Church Mission to Arabia, who was spending some time at Suk-el-Gharb in order to learn the special dialect of the Bedawin Arabs. This finally led to his joining the Arabian Mission at Aden. Meanwhile, he had not hesitated to avow his faith in the New Testament teachings wherever he went, but he did so with so much tact and so manifest a spirit of love that he escaped that violence of persecution which others would have soon encountered. The struggle between him and his father, a staunch old Moslem of great apparent sincerity and most unbending and fanatical intolerance, presents a touching chapter in the young man's life. Firmness in his adherence to the supreme truth of God, coupled with great filial reverence and affection were so blended that the father's heart was moved with manifest love. But at last, when he despaired of recalling his son from his supposed errors, the bitterness and cruelty of the Moslem faith asserted themselves and gave place to threats of death.

Kamil never returned, but as if feeling that his time was possibly short he devoted himself with most untiring assiduity to his work, laboring in season and out of season, whether he had an audience of a dozen or of one only. He thoroughly prepared himself by a study of the Koran at the same time that he studied earnestly the New Testament, and he was thus able, like the early apostles, to reason with his adversaries out of their own scriptures. Never since the example of the apostle Paul has there been an instance in which greater tact was shown in disarming prejudice and in opening the way for the truth. Passage after passage was shown to the incredulous in the Koran itself which commended the character of Christ, which quoted various passages of the Old Testament and the New, which instead of making it a crime to study the gospel, recommended it, and the relation of Christ to the Old Testament prophecy, which the Koran approved, was shown with such cogency that men came again and again to listen.

A bright and shining light indeed was this young missionary, this converted Moslem, voyaging from port to port along the Arabian coast, and finally adopting Busrah as the particular field of his labor. One is astonished at the favor and consideration which were given him even by Moslems, and that in the most fanatical of all lands. But, unfortunately, he encountered the Turkish soldiery at Busrah. With them nice comparisons of Koran and Gospel had little place or appreciation. Their creed was a short one, religiously and politically. Death to the apostate was the pithy conclusion of all that they believed or knew.

It is only necessary to add that Kamil died after a very brief and distressing illness, supposed to be the result of poison. He had survived but two years after his conversion. His rooms at Busrah were closed and sealed, an autopsy was refused, he was buried, contrary to his wishes, according to Moslem ceremony, and the place of his burial was concealed. The truth, however, which he had proclaimed could not be hidden, and in the minds and hearts of scores and even hundreds of staunch Moslems the seeds of the truth as it is in Jesus had been planted.

The story of this young man can not fail to be regarded as a valuable accession to the missionary literature of the day. First, it proves the utter falsity of the oracular assertion so often made by transient travelers, that no Moslem is ever converted to the Christian faith. We have never known clearer evidence of the genuineness of the work of the Spirit of God in connection with his truth. The transformation in Paul's life was scarcely clearer or more impressive.

Second, an admirable example is afforded to missionaries in heathen and Moslem lands, and indeed to preachers and evangelists at home as well, of that alert and ever wise tact which finds "the line of least resistance" to the heart and conscience of one's adversary. There are those who stoutly deny the necessity of learning anything whatever concerning the non-Christian religions, who deem it utter folly to study the Koran, even though one labors in Syria or Persia, and equally senseless to disturb the musty tomes of Buddhist or Hindu lore if one's field is India; all that is needed is the story of the Cross. This young Syrian did not thus believe. If he had been a student of the Koran before, there was tenfold necessity now, for it was upon the teachings of the Koran and the entire cult of Islam that he purposed to move with an untiring and fearless conquest. He would have to deal with men of intelligence and intellectual training, and if he would show the superiority of the gospel of Christ, he must know how to make an intelligent comparison. If he would inculcate the supreme truth, he must generously recognize any particles of truth already possessed. Paul on Mars hill before a heathen audience of Greeks, Paul before Agrippa, a ruler versed in the doctrines of the Jews, was not more wise and tactful than Kamil.

Third, if there were no other motive for studying this little sketch by Dr. Jessup, it is thrice valuable as a personal means of grace. Such a life of clear faith and of untiring devotion is tonic, and must be to every truly Christian heart.

Fourth, the life of Kamil affords another proof that the gospel has a universal application to the hearts of men, that it is indeed the wisdom of God and the power of God unto salvation, "to the Jew first, and also to the Gentile."

F. F. ELLINWOOD.

January 18, 1898.

A SKETCH OF THE LIFE
OF
KAMIL ABDUL MESSIAH EL AIETANY

On the morning of February 10, 1890, a young Syrian called at my study in Beirut. His face was unusually attractive and his manner courteous and winning. He soon handed me an Arabic letter he had written and taken to the Rev. Dr. Van Dyck, and on the back of which Dr. Van Dyck had indorsed his recommendations.

I read the letter carefully. The writer said in substance the following:

"After kissing your revered hands, your humble servant begs to state, my name is Kamil Aietany, of Beirut. I have studied Turkish and Arabic in the military schools and have been in government service in Beirut. For thirty days I have been to the Jesuit College seeking the salvation of my soul and to follow the Christian faith, according to clear and convincing proofs. They proposed to send me to Alexandria, but my father and brothers protested. I come now to you, regarding you in the place of father and brethren, asking your counsel as you are well known as a counselor of those who love learning, especially if they love learning more than father and family. Do with me as you please."

Dr. Van Dyck indorsed on this letter:

"I send this man to you. I have advised him to go to Egypt or India.

"C. V. A. VAN DYCK."

In reply to my questions, Kamil stated in the most frank and ingenuous manner that one day he met a young Maronite priest near the Beirut River, and on telling him he wished to learn French was advised to go to the Jesuit College. He went there and began to study. One of the fathers gave him an Arabic testament which he took home. His father saw him reading it, and, taking it from him, burned it in the kitchen fire. The next day one of the Jesuit teachers told him to take another New Testament and tell his father that he had bought it in order to write a tract attacking it; then his father would let him keep it. "I said to him, 'What! do you advise me to lie to my own father? Never!' And I laid down the book and came away."

Then he said to me: "Sir, I want to know just what you believe about Christ and the way of salvation. I am not at rest. I find nothing in the Koran to show me how God can be a just God and yet pardon a sinner. I know I am a sinner and that God is merciful, but he is also just."

There was a seriousness in his tone that showed him to be in earnest, and his language was so refined that I felt drawn to him at once. I said, "My dear friend, our only knowledge of Christ and the way of salvation is from the word of God, and here it is on the table—the Old and New Testaments. You can read for yourself. I will help you all I can. If your father objects to your taking a Bible home you are welcome to the use of my study daily as many hours as you wish. I am engaged at the Press every forenoon and you can occupy my study."

Then I opened the New Testament and

BEIRUT HARBOR—MT. LEBANON—JEBEL SUNNÎN, 8600 FEET HIGH.

read to him: "Come unto me, all ye that labor and are heavy laden, and I will give you rest." "Did Mohammed ever venture to use such language as that?" I asked. He said, "No." I then said, "Now, when you read the gospel ask yourself, Who was Jesus Christ? and why does he speak as if he were God? He says he will give us rest from sin and trouble and sorrow. He says, 'I and my Father are one.' 'I, if I be lifted up from the earth, will draw all men unto me.'"

Then I read other passages—from Acts 4: 12, "Neither is there salvation in any other; for there is none other name under heaven given among men, whereby we must be saved;" and from Rom. 5: 1, "Therefore, being justified by faith, we have peace with God through our Lord Jesus Christ."

Kamil listened intently to every word, and asked questions as if hungering and thirsting for the truth. Then he asked, "How do you pray?" I told him we would engage in prayer, asking divine grace and help and the guidance of the Spirit. He knelt by my side and repeated every word after me. At the close he said, "I never heard this kind of a prayer before. It is talking with God. We repeat words five times a day, but we have no such prayers as yours."

I then laid on the table the Bible, the Concordance, the Bible Handbook, and the Westminster Assembly's Shorter Catechism with proof texts. I explained to him that this Catechism was in men's words, but was concise and would give him an idea of the system of Christian belief, but he need not accept a word of it unless he could find it supported by the Scriptures. I also urged him to ask divine aid and light whenever he read the Bible, and then I left him alone. On returning at noon I found that he had prepared a series of questions about various passages of Scripture which he had been reading. These I explained to him.

On the evening of the next day he called and remained two hours. He had committed to memory the first ten answers of the Catechism. With the fourth, fifth, and sixth he was delighted. The answer, "God is a Spirit, infinite, eternal, and unchangeable, in his being, wisdom, power, holiness, justice, goodness, and truth," charmed him; and the sixth answer,— "There are three persons in the Godhead: the Father, the Son, and the Holy Ghost; and these three are one God, the same in substance, equal in power and glory,"—he said, set his mind at rest. "We Mohammedans think that the Christians worship three Gods," said he; "but you do not; for there is one God in three persons: the Eternal Father, the Eternal Word, and the Eternal Spirit. That is all clear." Then we read the Bible together for two hours and he listened with astonishment and delight. He seized upon the great doctrine of the atoning sacrifice of Christ with such eagerness and satisfaction that he seemed to be taught of the divine Spirit from the very outset. "This," he said, "is what we need. The Koran does not give us a way of salvation. It leaves us in doubt as to whether God will forgive our sins. It does not explain how he can do so and preserve his honor and justice. Here in the gospel it is plain. Christ bore our sins; he died in our stead; he died to save us from dying. This is beautiful; it is just what I want."

He then spoke of the Moslem claim that the Old and New Testaments have been tampered with and changed, and that when Mohammed commended the Old and New Testaments he referred to the original Scriptures which Christians have changed to prove their own doctrines. I went over the historical proofs of the genuineness and authenticity of the New Testament, and the fact that with the multiplicity of Christian sects it would have been impossible after the days of Mohammed to change the text of the Scriptures, as there was no central power whose authority was acknowleged by all, and that the New Testament in the hands of Protestants, Greeks, Roman Catholics, Armenians, and Copts is the same everywhere. Moreover, that the earliest manuscripts of the Greek text, which antedated Mohammed, are identical with that accepted by all the Christian sects.

In our conversation I alluded to the jealous care with which the Jews guarded the text of the Old Testament, counting every word and letter and vowel point. Kamil then told a Moslem story of Mohammed Ali, pasha of

American Mission Press, Church, Sunday-School, and Female Seminary at Beirut.

Egypt. The Coptic patriarch, in conversation with Mohammed Ali, consented to change a verse of the New Testament to please the viceroy; whereupon a little Moslem boy standing by told the pasha that God would wither his hand if he changed a single dummeh or fetha (vowel) or a single word in the Koran. Kamil then said it was probably in that spirit that the Jews and Christians have preserved God's Word intact.

On the 18th of February he spent the evening again with me and recited to the twenty-first question of the Catechism. The expression, "The only Redeemer of God's elect is the Lord Jesus Christ, who, being the eternal Son of God, became man," etc., was especially attractive to him, and he repeated it over and over. He offered prayer, and I was deeply affected by the childlike simplicity of his confession of sin and his pleading for pardon and acceptance with God in Christ.

It was a privilege to hear his exclamations of joy and pleasure as he read one chapter after another in the New Testament. It was all new to him and he drank it in as if he had found a cool crystal spring in a burning desert.

Again and again I wondered at his sincere and frank simplicity of character. He was a true Nathanael "in whom was no guile," and I thought to myself how wonderful that a young man brought up in a Moslem military school and surrounded by evil influences all his days, hearing cursing and foul language from old and young, should be so pure of life and so spiritual in his thoughts and language. The Arabic language is overloaded with religious expressions. The name of God is in constant use, in rising and sitting, in every act and motion, and on all occasions men say, "In the name of Allah," "If Allah will," "Praise to Allah," "O Allah," "I swear by the life of Allah," "Allah keep you," "The will of Allah be done," "Allah destroy your house," "Allah blight your life," "Allah curse your father," or "your grandfather." It is constant blessing or cursing from morning until night; and in addition there are expressions too vile to be translated, which the people use thoughtlessly and their children learn from them, and into which, even when in respectable society, they unconsciously fall. But Kamil seemed to have been kept from these habits, or to have broken them off at once and forever; for in all his subsequent life we never heard of his using improper language on any occasion.

His docility was striking. Day after day he called to read and join with me in prayer, and I was conscious of receiving a blessing whenever he came. He studied the various books carefully and took a little pocket Testament home with him.

On the 26th he had learned forty-two answers from the Catechism and soon finished it. He was greatly interested in the famous Arabic book, " The Letter of Abdul Messiah ibn Ishaak el Kindy " to his Moslem friend, the Hashimy, in the days of the caliph Mamûn, 800 A.D., inviting him to become a Christian. This book is regarded by the Moslems as so dangerous to their faith that they have a saying, " The house of any Moslem who shall possess the book shall be burned and also seventy houses around it."

Kamil took special comfort in the Gospel of John, and, when he returned home, would sit up late at night reading it. One morning his father listened at his door and heard him praying. Opening the door, he entered and said, "My son, what prayer is that you are using? You said, 'Our Father.' That is wrong. Have we not prayers enough without your using these prayers of the Christians?" Kamil told me that he said to his father, "My dear father, I was doing nothing wrong. God made us and loved us as you love me, and in this sense I say, 'Our Father.' I do not mean, as the Moslems think, that God was married and had children as men are and do. God forbid. It is only to express the tender relation between him and his children." But his father replied, "My son, we have prayers that are good enough without going to the Christians."

On Thursday, March 13th, Kamil came as usual. He said, "Last night my father kept me reading the Arabic Koran until midnight with the tajweed, so that I could not read any other book." The "tajweed" is a sonorous intoning of the words in reading, almost like

BASHURA QUARTER OF BEIRUT—MOSQUE ATTENDED BY KAMIL'S FAMILY.

chanting, of which the Moslems are extremely fond, and is not unlike the intoning of the Greek priests and Jewish rabbis. On this occasion I again urged him to be careful not to wound the feelings of his aged father. "Remember that he is your father," said I, "that he loves you; and never forget the respect and affection due to him." "I never will," he replied; and in all his intercourse and subsequent correspondence he showed his love and reverence for his father, who is a venerable sheikh, and the leader in several circles or halakas of the Zikr.* He is looked upon as a most devout Moslem.

---

* Zikr is, literally, "remembering,"—*i.e.*, remembering God, —and consists in repeating the name of God, "Allah," hundreds and thousands of times. It is either "jali," recited aloud, or "khafi," recited with a low voice or mentally.

As a religious ceremony or act of devotion it is performed by the various religious orders of Faqirs or Darweshes all over the Mohammedan world. Almost every religious Moslem is a member of one of these orders, and their meetings, in which they stand in a ring, are called "Halakat ez Zikr," or circle of remembrance of the name of God.

In one zikr khafi they repeat the words, "God the Hearer," "God the Seer," "God the Knower," and then "la ilaha," "there is no God," with the exhalation of the breath, and with each inhalation "illa 'llahu," "excepting God." This style of zikr is a most exhausting act, being performed hundreds

Kamil had now been for a month under almost daily instruction, and had decided deliberately to profess Christianity and devote his life to preaching Christ to the Mohammedans. It was important that he have systematic religious instruction, and it became a serious question as to where this could best be secured.

---

and even thousands of times, beginning slowly and ending with fearful rapidity, until often the devotees sink exhausted on the floor.

The following, used by the Qadiriyah devotees, is considered the most devotional and spiritual by the Moslem mystics:

1. He (God) is first. He is last. The manifest and the hidden, and who knoweth all things.
2. He is with you wheresoever ye be.
3. We (God) are closer to man than his neck-vein.
4. Whichever way ye turn, there is the face of God.
5. God encompasseth all things.
6. All on earth shall pass away, but the face of thy God shall abide resplendent with majesty and glory.

There is much of superstition connected with this devotional exercise. The Chishtiyah order believe that if a man sits cross-legged and seizes the vein called Kaimas, which is under the leg, with his toes, it will give peace to his heart, when accompanied by a repetition of the "Kalimah," "There is no deity but God."

The most common form of zikr is the recital of the ninety-nine names of God: as "the Merciful, the Great, the King, the Mighty, the Compassionate, the Wise, the Strong, the Forgiver, the Opener," etc.

There are other forms, as the "Tasbih," "Praise be to God"; "Tahmid," "Thanks, or Glory be to God"; and

About ten miles from Beirut, on a spur of the Mount Lebanon range, at an altitude of twenty-five hundred feet above the sea, is the village of Suk-el-Gharb, where is the American Boarding School for Boys, under the care of the Rev. Mr. Hardin. As Kamil knew the Turkish

---

"Takbir," "God is Great." Mohammed said, "Repeat the 'Tasbih' a hundred times, and a thousand virtues shall be recorded by God for you, ten virtuous deeds for each repetition."

Mr. John P. Brown, in his history of the Darweshes (Dervishes: Persian, Dar, house, as they beg from house to house), says that they are divided into thirty-two orders. He says that in one of their ceremonies, after working themselves into a religious delirium, "they burn themselves with red-hot irons, gloat upon them tenderly, lick them, bite them, hold them between their teeth, and end by cooling them in their mouths. Those who are unable to procure any seize with fury upon the cutlasses hanging on the wall and stick them into their sides and legs." However severely they may be burned or wounded, they believe that their sheikh can heal them by breathing on them and rubbing them with saliva.

Among the sayings ascribed to Mohammed are the following: "Let your tongue be always moist in the remembrance of God." "There are ninety-nine names of God; whosoever counts them up shall enter into Paradise." "The ejaculation, 'There is no power and strength but in God', is medicine for ninety-nine pains, the least of which is melancholy." "No one can bring a better deed on the day of resurrection (unless he shall have said the like or added to it) than he who has recited, 'Oh, Holy God. Praise be to Thee', one hundred times every morning and evening."

No doubt it was such "vain repetitions" as these against which Christ warned his disciples.

language, it was arranged that he go to Suk and teach Turkish in the boys' school, and receive instruction in the Bible. His father consented, and on March 20th he left Beirut for his new post. His progress in the forty days of his Bible study and conversation in Beirut had been remarkable. The most spiritual portions of the New Testament had become familiar to him. Prayer seemed his special delight. I have never met a person who, from the outset, seemed so peculiarly taught of the Spirit of God.

On his entering the school at Suk as teacher of Turkish, the boys of the Protestant and Oriental Christian sects looked on him with suspicion. They said, "This man is a Beirut Mohammedan, and who knows but he is immoral and will corrupt his companions?" But his consistent Christian life and pure language and his zeal in studying the Scriptures soon overcame all prejudice, and he was chosen leader in the religious meetings of the boys. From that time his course was onward and upward. It is the testimony of Mr. Hardin and the native instructors that they never have had a more truly devout and pure young man in the school. He wrote to me frequently asking advice and telling me of his affairs. On April 17th he wrote of his beginning to teach Turkish. In this letter he speaks of his first acquaintance with the Rev. James Cantine, then in Suk studying Arabic in preparation for missionary work in Arabia. As Kamil's letter is a characteristic Arabic epistle, I will translate it literally, but in subsequent letters, for brevity's sake, I shall omit the flowery introduction.

"Suk-el-Gharb to Beirut,
"17, Nisan (April), 1890.

"To his excellency, his presence, my lord and spiritual father, Dr. Henry Jessup the revered, may God prolong his continuance in honor and divine favor, Amen.

"After kissing your dear hands and asking your prayers always, I would state that in the most blessed time and most favored hour we were honored by your precious letter. We read it and praised the Creator (be he exalted) for your health and peace, which we always pray for to the Lord of all creatures. In this letter you told us of the Rev. Mr. Cantine, who is planning to go to Yemen, if God wills. Be it

PANORAMA OF SYRIAN PROTESTANT COLLEGE BUILDINGS IN BEIRUT.

Panorama of Syrian Protestant College Buildings in Beirut.

known to you, therefore, that already a strong affection has grown up between us, so that he is now giving me a nightly lesson in translating from the Arabic Gospel of John into English, in Mr. Hardin's house. I am exceedingly grateful to you for making me acquainted with this cultivated and excellent man. He has overwhelmed me with his kindness and many favors. I pray God to prosper him according to his good intentions. I have received the kind advice contained in your letter, which is 'Bless and curse not' and 'Bless them that curse you,' and thank you for it. If it be God's will I will never, from this time on, curse my enemies. Do not fail to give me good religious advice whenever you write.

"I am about to teach Turkish, for I feel that if one has mastered any branch of knowledge and does not use it it will be like a lost treasure.

"The Lord bless and prosper you, and bless you in health and the peace of his dear Son, our Lord and Saviour Jesus Christ, Amen. Do not forget me in your prayers for me, that my heart may increase in light upon light.

"And may you abide in peace.

"Y'r servant, penitent for his sins,

"Kamil Abdul Messiah (servant of Christ).

"P. S.—Give my best salaams to every member of your household, though I do not know their names. The Lord guard and preserve them through all this life. Amen.

"Mr. Hardin and Mr. Cantine salute you. Our brother Jedaan Owad, the Bedawi, salutes you. Written in haste, please excuse the writing."

During the next three months he continued his studies and teaching. As the summer vacation drew near he was anxious for some sphere of Christian work in which he could be useful to his countrymen. His father had written to him expressing great love for him and at the same time deep anxiety at rumors he had heard of Kamil's having become a Christian. One of his letters was eloquent and most touching, entreating him not to bring down his aged father's gray hairs with sorrow to the grave. Kamil replied affectionately, but saying that he was trying to please God and do his will and fit himself for usefulness.

In July he thought that he would better not return to Beirut, lest some of the lower class of fanatical Moslems might take his life.

The young Bedawi, Jedaan, whose salutations he sent me, was a fellow-pupil and a warm friend of Kamil's, and after conference and prayer it was decided that they should go together on a preaching tour for the summer among the Bedawin Arab tribes in the vicinity of Hamath and Hums, along the river Orontes.

In the Summer of 1887 Jedaan had come with a flock of sheep from the plains west of Palmyra to Mount Lebanon, and spent several months in Suk-el-Gharb selling his sheep. He came from one of the branches of the powerful Anazy tribe of nomadic Arabs, among the thousands of which tribe there was hardly a man able to read or write. One day Jedaan passed a man in a wayside shop reading. He stopped and asked, "Can a Bedawi learn to read?" The man said, "Yes; any one can learn." Jedaan (Gideon) became greatly interested, and the man sent him to Mr. Ibrahim Ahtiyeh, a Protestant teacher of the British Syrian Schools in Beirut, who was summering at his house in Suk. Mr. Ahtiyeh gave him an Arabic alphabet card, and he began at once to learn his letters. Day after day he studied his alphabet while leading his sheep to pasture on the mountain near the village, and was con-

Bedawin Women and Children of the Anazy Tribe.

stantly asking the passers-by the name and sound of the Arabic letters and simple words. By the end of the summer he was able to read simple sentences, and became possessed with the desire to learn more. When in the neighboring village of Aitath one day, he met a Druze sheikh of the village and a Mohammedan effendi of one of the leading families of Beirut, and told them he wished to learn Arabic. They advised him to go to the English school in Beirut; and thus unconsciously these two Syrian gentlemen put him in the way of finding not only a knowledge of the Arabic language, but of the word of God and the way of life. He sent back the money received for the sheep, by his Bedawi companion, who returned to join the tribe before its annual migration eastward down the Euphrates, telling him to inform his uncle, the sheikh of the tribe, that he had remained in order to learn reading, writing, and arithmetic, so as to be useful to his tribe in the future.

Mrs. Mentor Mott, to whom he applied for admission to her boys' school in Beirut, received him cordially, and he became an inmate of the family of **Mr.** Ibrahim Ahtiyeh. **I** noticed him in the Sunday-school and **at** church, and by degrees became acquainted with **him.** The **Christian** religion was **at** first strange **and mysterious to him.** The Bedawin Arabs are simple monotheists, and, **though** regarded by the government as Mohammedans, have no religious **sheikhs or** imams, no **places of worship, and no** hours of prayer, and rarely keep the fast **of** Ramadan or make the pilgrimage to Mecca. **So the Moslems say: "There are** three classes **who have no religion, muleteers,** Bedawin Arabs, **and women,"** because they do not observe the ritual **of Islam.**

As Jedaan read the New Testament in Arabic, and attended divine service and the Sunday-school, the light began gradually to break into his mind. But it was not until he **had been under** instruction **a** year and four months that **he** finally accepted the Christian faith and **asked for** baptism. He was urged **to count** the **cost and** consider well what that **step involved.** But he had made up his mind deliberately, **and was** baptized February 21, 1889. His faith **was simple and** clear, and he seemed anxious to fit himself not only to write letters and keep accounts for his tribe, but to teach them the word of God and the religion of Jesus Christ. He entered the school in Suk-el-Gharb in October, and was among the first to welcome Kamil on his arrival. They had much in common, and were soon as warmly attached as David and Jonathan. It was Jedaan who proposed that they go on their preaching tour to all the Arab encampments around Hums and Hamath, including that of his own tribe.

On July 28th they called on me in Aaleih, Mount Lebanon, about two miles from Suk, *en route* for the North. They said they had come to bid me good-by and ask my prayers for a blessing on their journey. After I had offered prayer, each of them prayed most earnestly for divine aid and invoked God's blessing on me, on all my family, and on all the missionaries in Syria. It was very affecting to hear the voices of this son of the desert and this young Mohammedan, both so recently born into the kingdom of grace, praying with such simple, intelligent faith and loving gratitude.

They went on to Zahleh and Baalbec and thence through the northern Bukaa to the great plains dotted with the black goats'-hair tents of the Bedawin. They went from encampment to encampment, receiving the free hospitality of the Arabs, welcomed everywhere. They read to the Arabs from the Old and New Testaments, and preached salvation through Jesus Christ. They wrote letters for the sheikhs, helped them in their accounts, and urged them to give up their predatory raids and robberies and to live in the fear of God. One sheikh said : "This may do for dwellers in towns, but if Arabs rob us we must punish them by robbing them." The *lex talionis* has been the Arabs' rule since the days of their father Ishmael.

The two zealous young disciples spent two months in the Bedawin camps. Kamil said on his return that Jedaan had the advantage of him in knowing the pure Bedawi pronunciation and idioms, and Jedaan said that at times he felt very timid lest the Arabs injure them for speaking of Christ, but that Kamil was bold as a lion.

In the latter part of September they returned and gave a full account of their journey. They had been in every camp for miles east, west, north, and south of Hamath, and had read the Scriptures to hundreds of Arabs, sowing good seed that may yet spring up to the glory of God. Kamil brought as a present to my family a beautiful live bird, a rail, or blue heron, which he got in the Bukaa near Baalbec. He said he brought it as a thank-offering, because he had been permitted to accomplish this journey in safety.

After completing their Bedawin labors they came into the city of Hums one Saturday to spend the Sabbath. Taking a room in a khan in the quarter of the Greek weavers, they called on the Protestant pastor. The news soon spread through the city that a young Beirut Mohammedan who had become a Christian was in the khan. Toward evening five young Syrian weavers of the Greek sect called upon them in the khan, curious to see a Moslem convert to Christianity. After the usual polite salutations they began to ply Kamil with questions as to his name, and whether it was actually true that he had become a Christian. He said, "Certainly." They asked, "How did it come about?" "By reading God's word and by prayer," he replied. "Are you a member of the Orthodox Apostolic Greek Church?" they then asked. "I don't find the name of any such church in the Bible," said he. They then began with great zeal to try to convince him that he should be baptized by a Greek priest and should believe in prayers to the saints and to the Virgin, and in the doctrine of transubstantiation. Kamil took out his Arabic Testament and began to explain to them the doctrine of free salvation and of justification by faith, with the most tender earnestness. Then standing up he offered prayer for them all, and when he had finished they were all in tears. They thanked him and went away, full of wonder that a Moslem convert should have to show them the way of salvation through Christ alone. The next morning they all went to the Protestant church and proposed to be enrolled as Protestants. News of this was carried to the Greek bishop, Athanasius Ahtullah. This bishop is one of the most enlightened of the Greek clergy in Syria. When a lad, he attended the Protestant common school in Suk, and he has opened large and well-conducted schools in Hums, with 1200 pupils; and the Bible printed at the American Press is used as a text-book in them all. He sent and invited Kamil to visit him. On Kamil's arrival in the large reception room, the bishop sent out all the priests and servants and brought Kamil to the raised divan at the upper end of the room, and, seating him at his right hand, saluted him most cordially. On learning his family name, the bishop said: "I know of your family and am glad you have become a Christian." Then he began to urge him to enter the Orthodox Greek Church, and used the usual arguments of the traditional oriental Christians. Kamil asked, "What does Your Excellency believe about Christ? Is he a perfect and sufficient Saviour?" The bishop said, "Yes." "Do you believe, as St. Paul says, that, 'being justified by faith, we have peace with God through our Lord Jesus Christ?'" "Yes," replied the bishop. "Then," said Kamil, "we are brethren in belief; and what more do we want?" But the bishop urged him to accept trine immersion at the hands of a true priest of the Apostolic Orthodox Greek Church, and then he would be all right. Then Kamil, turning to the bishop, said, "Your Excellency, supposing that you and I were traveling west from Hums and came to the river Orontes; and the river was deep, muddy, swift, and broad; and there was neither bridge nor boat, and neither of us could swim. Then if I should say to you, 'Bishop, I beg you to take me across.' What would you say? You would say, 'Kamil I can not take myself across, and how can I take you?' And there we would stand helpless and despairing. But suppose that just then we should see a huge giant, a strong, tall man, coming toward us, and he should take you by the arms and carry you across. Would I call out, 'Bishop, come and take me across'? No; I would call to the strong man. Bishop, there is only one strong Man—the Lord Jesus Christ. Is not he enough?" Turning to Kamil, the bishop asked, "My dear friend, how long have you been a Christian?" "Seven months," was the reply. "Seven months! And you are teaching me who have been a Christian in name from my infancy. Kamil, you are right. If you will stay here and teach Turkish in my school I will pay you a higher salary than you can get in any school in Syria." "Your Excellency," replied Kamil, "I thank you for your offer; but I care not for money or salary. God has called me to preach the gospel to the Mohammedans, and I must complete my studies and be about my work."

I shall never forget the truly eloquent and affecting manner in which he described this interview with the bishop of Hums. It showed how completely he was imbued with the spirit of faith and Christian love, and how his exquisite courtesy and sweetness of disposition disarmed all opposition.

Kamil and Jedaan returned to the Suk school and resumed their studies. Kamil's religious influence continued undiminished and he took part heartily in all religious meetings. Mr. Hardin states that it was refreshing to see how new and striking were his views and applications of gospel truth.

In October he wrote to me of his welfare and stated that the Greek priest in Suk had offered to teach him Greek in order to help him understand the New Testament, but his studies and his teaching of Turkish left him no time to take up Greek. Some of the monks of Deir Shir, a papal Greek monastery near Suk, made several attempts to persuade him to become a Romanist, but he finally told them they would better preach to the Moslems than attempt to pervert a Christian believer to Romish tradition and superstition.

Early in January he wrote to me again asking for certain books, and closed by saying, " We have been reading Acts 8 : 36–40, and would ask, ' Who shall forbid that I be baptized ? ' "

Up to this time he had been on probation, and it was thought better to give him time to take the step deliberately. But now there seemed no reason for further delay. He was rooted and grounded in the faith of Jesus Christ, and he was baptized January 15th, rejoicing thus to take his stand decidedly for Christ, his Saviour.

The Rev. James Cantine and the Rev. Samuel

M. Zwemer had been spending some months in Beirut and Suk-el-Gharb studying the Arabic in preparation for their mission to Arabia. The idea of this mission was conceived by Prof. Lansing, of the Theological Seminary, New Brunswick, New Jersey. Having been born in Egypt, and being a fine Arabic scholar, he was deeply interested in the welfare of the Mohammedans of Arabia. The Rev. Keith Falconer had fallen at his post soon after beginning his work in Aden, and the Free Church of Scotland was keeping up the work there, but Dr. Lansing planned entering Arabia from all sides and offering a free gospel and a divine Saviour to its millions of people. In the closing months of 1890 Messrs. Cantine and Zwemer left Beirut for Aden, and soon wrote requesting Kamil to join them there; so, without delay, after his baptism, he came to Beirut, and, making the necessary preparations, sailed for Port Said, the northern terminus of the Suez Canal, arriving in Aden February 7, 1891. He was heartily welcomed by the missionaries and began his work at once among the Arabs. Aden is the seaport of southern Arabia, and caravans of Arabs from the mountains north toward Sanaa and east toward Hadramout are constantly coming in, bringing coffee, dates, spices, and wool, and buying European goods. It was to these caravans that the missionaries recommended Kamil to give his attention, and he

THE PORT OF ADEN.

did so day after day. He often had from fifty to one hundred Arabians seated around him listening to the word of God.

On March 18, 1891, he made his first missionary journey with Mr. Zwemer along the southern coast of Arabia. He carefully wrote a journal in Arabic, which I received May 20th.

The following is the substance of the journal, in his own language:

"Our blessed journey to Bender-el-Makullah. 'And they departed, and went through the towns, preaching the gospel, and healing everywhere,' Luke 9: 6. After trusting in God and asking the aid of his Holy Spirit, I set out with my beloved and zealous brother, Mr. Zwemer, from Aden on Saturday, March 18, 1891, at half-past four o'clock in the night [10.30 P. M.]. We sailed in a sloop sixty feet in length, intending to visit Bender-el-Makullah. The name of the ship was 'Mubarakat' [the blessed], and the captain's name was Es Sayyid Omr Najy. The ship had one mast, and it had on board, including passengers and sailors, twenty-five souls, and was bound to Belhaf, east of Aden.

"The next day, March 19th, owing to severe seasickness, we were unable to speak to any one. On the 20th we began to make the acquaintance of the sailors, the captain, and the passengers, and came to be on friendly terms with them all, and tried to draw their hearts to us personally. On the 21st love sprang up in their hearts and they listened gladly. We then spoke to them kindly and freely about the gospel, in such a way as to prevent their being shocked or repelled, so that they bought two Bibles. We showed the divine authority and inspiration of the gospel, bringing proofs from the Koran, and they bought the books with all joy. In the sea [Arabic idiom for during] of that day we stopped at the little village of Shefra, where there is good water, and then sailed on to the east, and, as the wind was contrary, the ship anchored at night and sailed at dawn. On Wednesday, the 22d, I read to the men a portion, using the tajweed, [or loud musical intoning with which the Moslems read the Koran]. They listened with rapt attention and delight, and whenever I paused they shouted to me to go on. At evening we passed Azam. On Thursday, the 23d, I took a portion of the sailors, and Mr. Zwemer the rest, and we spoke to them of the plan of salvation, of the prophecies of the Old Testament prophets of the coming of our Saviour to the world, and we told them plainly that we are Christians and worship God (be he praised and exalted!), the Creator of the heavens and the earth, until it was made clear to them that Christians are not infidels (kafirs) if they thus believe. [It is the custom in all this region to call all others than Mohammedans kafirs.] At the end of every sentence they responded, 'Zein, zein, wallah zein; laisoo b'kuffar,'—' Very fine; by the name of Allah, fine; they are not kafirs.' They greatly delighted in our teaching, and we set apart a special time daily to instruct them about the way of salvation. As we sailed along the coast we saw numerous mountains to the north far greener than the mountains of Aden. We asked whether there were men living on them, and the reply was, 'Yes; they are like the sands which

ADEN CUSTOM HOUSE AND LANDING PLACE.

can not be counted or numbered, and they are ruled by many sultans who are at perpetual war, and peace is only secured in the end by the aid of the kadis [judges]. The water is chiefly rain-water, and fountains of living water are scarce.' At evening we passed Mukatein, and on Friday, the 23d, we were at Hur, a little hamlet, and saw a mountain white as snow, called 'Zooaij al

Akezim,' in which men are said to be as plentiful as locusts. In front of this mountain is a litoral called 'Jurd Takhumah.' We then saw Sheikha, Harba, Rida, and Jaal, names of plains thinly inhabited. On Saturday, the 25th, we were at Arkah, the town of sheikh Abdurahman el Badas and the site of his tomb. The Arabs regard him as one of the holy saints. Two of the people came to us and we asked them, 'Do you know the Injeel [the gospel], and have you heard about the Christ?' They replied, 'We have never heard of the Christ, nor do we know what the gospel is.' We then told them briefly about Christ and the gospel and salvation and many other things, and they listened with deep interest, so that we begged the captain to stop longer, but he refused for two reasons: firstly, for want of time, and, secondly, as the harbor is unsafe. The town has a well of good water and a little way from it is an ancient fortress. On Sunday, the 26th, we were at Ras Hoora and Sufan. The Bedawin sing a song about these places and Ras Arka as follows:

> 'No grass in Ras Hoora, in Sufan not a taint,
> But Ras Arka would make of a rebel a saint.'

That is, Ras Hoora and Sufan are of no profit, though they have a market and many people, but Ras Arka is safe and its people are honest.

"On Sunday we also reached Ghubt-el-Ain, and on Monday, the 27th, Belhaf, the destination of our ship and passengers. We bade a very affectionate good-by to the sailors and captain, and sold them six Arabic Testaments, they paying the price.

"We then entered Belhaf, a little village, a market for goods landed here for the Arabs in the interior. It has neither water nor vegetation, indeed nothing but a fortress and houses of straw. The people are like stones. They do not like strangers and will not give them even water, except for money. While we were there four sultans of the Bedawin were in town. Our brother Zwemer gave medicine to ten sick people and asked for a little coffee or milk. But why speak to one who is lifeless? I then told the sultans about the Bedawin Arabs in Syria; how the very poor among them entertain every stranger that comes, and how they give him food and drink and the best they have, with other remarks intended to appeal to their self-respect and their sense of shame. But alas! it all went for nothing, so that one of the sultans who was sick sent for Mr. Zwemer, and when Mr. Zwemer asked him for a little leben [curdled milk], promising to give him medicine without charge, as he did to the others, the sultan said he would do without both healing and medicine sooner than give one piaster's worth of leben. (Just think of that, sir!) We found ourselves here shut up like Peter and Paul in prison, and although we preached to them of the salvation through Christ and offered to sell them books, who among such a people would listen to us? I presented one Testament to the owner of the house where we lodged, and on the morning of Tuesday, March 28th, we took passage in a little boat nine yards long. It had three captains: one for the rudder, one for the sail, and one to bail out the water, which kept coming in from the sea. We set sail after offering prayer to God, but our sailors were like deaf-and-dumb men with no understanding. For instance, they insisted that we transfer our baggage and clothing to another boat, as it was too heavy for the ship to carry, though after a hot contest they gave up the demand and submitted. But after we had sailed a little way, lo! the ship drew near the land, and two of the captains went ashore and brought huge stones and put them in for ballast, as the cargo was too light. (Just think of it, sir!) After much tribulation we reached Beer Ali, a little village with excellent water and a people somewhat better than those of Belhaf, for they helped us in preparing food and offered us a place to sleep, but with many thanks we declined and slept in the boat. There is a fortress near here and the people say there are inscriptions. We asked whether they were Arabic, English, or French. They said neither, but in the language of the Franks, and thus displayed their great knowledge. The castle is lofty, but was too distant for us to visit it. At dawn on the 29th we left Beer Ali and in the morning saw Mejdaha, a little village of ten houses and a spring of water. On our course we saw numerous islands, and on rounding them the winds rose and the waves dashed over us on every side, the boat pitching and rolling until we and our books and clothing and the sail and the sailors were drenched. We shivered in the biting cold, and four or six times death stared us in the face. We were in a sad state and protected ourselves with prayer and singing praises, and in supplication to God that he would look upon us in compassion. My brother, Mr. Zwemer, comforted me by recalling the sufferings of Christ, and I comforted him with the prisons and the sufferings of the apostles. At length we all agreed to run ashore and land until the storm should abate and the waves subside. So after much toil and tribulation we drew the boat up on the beach, and, owing to severe hunger, I began to prepare some food.

Just then there came up an armed Bedawi with a long spear. He saluted us and we responded.

He then said, 'You would better not stop in this wilderness; it is full of godless Bedawin, who will kill you or rob you of everything.' We replied, 'We fear nothing, for God is with us and we are his disciples; and "if God be for us, who can be against us?"' He said nothing and went on his way, but after five minutes returned with another Bedawi armed to the teeth. They saluted us and we answered with all courtesy and respect. They demanded coffee as rent of the land we stood on. We told them, 'We have no coffee; but if you wish dates you are most welcome.' They refused and demanded coffee five or six times, until finally they said they would take money instead. We refused to give money. Just then a crowd of Bedawin women and children came down upon us. Alas! how can we answer these robbers? How can we hold back this rabble of women and children who are clutching at our clothing and food? Sometimes a child seized one thing and a woman another, and four or five at once reached out their hands. The robbers kept talking and we answering, until Mr. Zwemer took his stand by one part of our things and I by another. I then called out, 'We have no coffee and we will not give money; but look out for yourselves, for I have something here in my heart which will preserve me, though you were as many as the sands on the seashore, for my conscience rests on the Lord Jesus Christ, and the Khowaja who is with me has a little thing which can kill five or six in the twinkling of an eye.' But it was as though I was talking to dead men, for they seized the boat and refused to let us launch it again. We then demanded their help at once, and we all took hold and drew the boat down to the water with all our goods. Mr. Zwemer then went up to the chief robber and cut off a little bead which was hanging from his neck, as a keepsake, and the man never uttered a word. Mr. Zwemer then gave him a cup as a token of remembrance and gave them all medicine for their ailments. We then took their spears and stuck their shafts into the ground and stood, with the Bedawin around us. I then offered prayer to God that he would enlighten their hearts and reform their lives and guide and save them. I prayed nearly half an hour, praying to God and then exhorting them, and I will venture to say with all joy that the Holy Spirit spoke, not I, for my eyes and my body and all my members were transfixed toward heaven, and from the very depths of my heart I prayed and preached. And I closed my prayer with the words ' In the name and for the honor of the Lord Jesus Christ, our Redeemer and our Saviour.' And the whole company responded,

'Amen and Amen'; and they exclaimed, 'Never in all our lives will we cut off the roads, rob on the highway again, or speak harshly to a stranger.' We then bade them a loving farewell and they said, ' Ma-es-Salameh,'—' Go in peace; may God preserve you.' We thanked them kindly and sailed on our way. But all this time our captain and sailors were like blocks of wood; they neither spoke nor moved. But when we sailed away a great fear of us came over them, and they said, 'Sirs, if anything happens to you we will give our lives for you.' We thanked them most cordially for this wonderful zeal, which had just no meaning at all. Mr. Zwemer said to me as we sailed away that he was filled with astonishment and joy at the prayer offered by the spears among the Bedawin.

"The wind continued to increase and we were truly water in water, and at length the captain said we would better go back to Beer Ali, and the next day set sail for El Makullah. We consented, and turning to Mr. Zwemer I said, 'My brother, God no doubt intends some greater things for us and has sent his Spirit to turn us back to his work.' He said he had no doubt of that. At length after great weariness and cold, hunger and thirst, we returned to Beer Ali. There we found a large vessel bound for El Makullah and decided that it would be better to take passage in it. So I went to the ship with our first captain, Mr. Zwemer enjoining him to help me in getting moderate rates for our passage. We went on board and met the captain, and we began to arrange about the fare, but our friend, the first captain, being offered dates to eat, forgot all about helping me and gave himself up to eating dates, saying, ' Every goat is hung up by his own leg,'—*i. e.*, every man for himself; and when I asked him to help me in the bargaining, he replied by taking more dates and filling his mouth.

"At length, on Wednesday evening, April 1st, we set sail. We at once made friends with the captain and his sailors and company owing to their courtesy and good manners. They were from Muscat and bound to that city, and they helped us in every way and seemed fond of us. They were forty in number, and when the morning of the 2d dawned all who were sick or ailing thronged around Mr. Zwemer, and all who wanted books thronged around me, especially when I had proved to them from the Koran that the Tourah and the Injeel [Old and New Testaments] are the books of God. They accepted the proofs and agreed that they were indeed from God, and in two days they had purchased thirty Bibles and Testaments. I spoke to them openly of the salvation in

Christ, and they listened attentively, saying to one another, 'Of a truth these are good men and their doctrine is light upon light,' insomuch that we were astonished at their ready acquiescence in our teaching, and we thanked God for this joyous work. When we prayed at morning and evening and at our meals, we spoke in a loud voice so that all could hear, and they listened in silence and were filled with wonder.

"Before prayer I always read a portion from the Gospels in the tajweed tone used in reading the Koran. This caused them great delight and drew them nearer and nearer to us. From that day love for us was planted in their hearts. They loved us and we loved them exceedingly. They continually brought us of their food and drink and whatever else we needed or asked for, and they were not a little civilized in their habits and conduct.

"On Friday, April 3d, two of them came to me and asked me to write out for them prayers for morning and evening and for use before eating. These prayers contained a petition that God would enlighten their hearts, that they might know him truly more and more, that he would send his Holy Spirit, his grace, and his word, and implant them in their hearts. I also wrote in them the Lord's Prayer and various spiritual expressions, closing by asking an

Aden Camel Market.

answer from God in honor of the Son of his love, the Lord Jesus Christ. These were written in a style which the Moslems admire, and when I read them to them they rejoiced exceedingly and thanked me for writing them. I then offered prayer to God, praising him for his mercies and for helping me in proclaiming the glad tidings of salvation. Then I recalled the word which I spoke to Mr. Zwemer, about our being turned back for a greater work, for so it was, yea even greater than we had supposed. To God be the thanks and the praise.

"On Saturday morning, April 4th, we reached Bender-el-Makullah, our destination. We bade farewell to the captain and his company with all affection, and they reverently entreated us to come to their city of Muscat, and we promised to come if the Spirit should permit. They were deeply affected and so were we, and at our parting we bade them God-speed with all joy in our hearts.

"On landing we went to the sultan and he gave us a house for a lodging during our stay. At noon the people began to come to us. I told them that Mr. Zwemer would give them medicine freely for the love of God, and that I would sell them books at a very low rate. The sick then came to Mr. Zwemer, and he gave them medicine and I sold books.

"On Sunday, April 5th, a company of boys came and took books, and when they went to their teacher he was greatly enraged, telling them to burn the books and buy no more. When the news reached me I sent for the teacher, and he came, bringing with him a second teacher and a third man. When they were seated I saluted them cordially and said, 'Oh, honored teachers, I have called you to take counsel and ask you about a very important matter and to tell you something new. If you find it to be true, help me to carry it out; if it be not true, teach me a better way, and if it be a true way, I will be very much obliged to you.' They replied, 'Speak, and we are your hearers.' I thanked them for their kindness and in the first place read to them from the Koran in the tone of the tajweed, and they were very much astonished at my knowing the tajweed and seemed delighted with my reading. When I finished I said to them, 'My father, my grandfather, and my great-grandfather were all of them Moslems. My father performed the pilgrimage to Mecca three times and my brothers have all been on the pilgrimage, and I am not a kafir. The difference between me and them is that I read the Tourah and the Injeel and believe in all that they say, and walk according to their divine commandments. For the Koran commands me to read them with reverence and regard, and confirms their inspiration, and if I do not read them I violate the command of God. Be he praised and exalted.' I then opened the Koran in proof of my words, and read to them four passages which enforce the reading of the Bible, as follows:

"Sura 5, Maida, v. 72: 'Oh, people of the Book, ye rest on nought until you stand fast by the Law and the Gospel and what is revealed to your Lord.'

"Sura 7, Inam, v. 156: 'Who follows the apostles, the illiterate prophet, whom they find written down with them in the Law (Tourah) and the Gospel (Injeel).'

"Sura 57:27: 'We gave him Jesus, the Gospel, and we placed in the hearts of those who followed him kindness and compassion.'

"Sura 5:110: 'When I taught thee the Book and Wisdom and the Law and the Gospel.'

"Then I said, 'Does this Koran speak truth or falsehood?' They said, 'Allah forbid that it should speak falsehood.' I said, 'Are my words true?' They replied 'Yes; there is no doubt of it.' 'Then,' said I, 'Why did you forbid the boys buying the books?' They said, 'We did not,' and denied it absolutely. I then said, 'You should buy the books if my words are true.' They said, 'We certainly will after hearing the proofs you have given us.' From that day the boys thronged around us and bought the Scriptures. The Moslems became very fond of me and invited me to act as muezzin and call to prayer from the minaret; but I excused myself, telling them that I by the grace of God am a Christian. They continued to visit me and I taught them as the Holy Spirit taught me to speak.

"On Monday, the 6th, Mr. Zwemer went to the house of a man who was very ill, near to death, with dropsy of the abdomen. Mr. Zwemer tapped the watery tumor and drew off the water, to the relief of the patient. I then kneeled with Mr. Zwemer at the sick man's feet and prayed to God, asking that he would answer us in honor of the Son of his love, the Lord Jesus Christ. The women and the men and children who had assembled all responded 'Amen' at the end of every sentence of my prayer. They bought a Bible and received it with joy, and we went forth thanking God.

"In every place and in every house which we entered we read the Lord's Prayer, with the tajweed, and sang hymns, and they rejoiced, and at the close responded with us, 'Amen.'

"El Makullah is a large town and finely paved, with many large houses four and five stories high and very well built. On the right of the town there are multitudes of Bedawin tents. There is a well of sulphur water and another of excellent sweet water. Vegetables are brought from the interior and are abundant and cheap. The cultivated district is small, owing to its being crowded by the mountains. The population is about seven thousand or more. There are mosques, but neither Jews nor Christians; so that we were a wonder to them. A steamer calls there three times a year, but sailing craft are numerous. There are sheep and cattle, camels and donkeys, and nearly everything. A little girl will wear in her ears as many as twenty rings, in her nose three, on her ankles two anklets of silver, and on her neck six strings of beads. They have many customs which it is not our province to describe. There are a few Hindus, to whom I went and sold Bibles.

"On Tuesday, April 7th, at evening, we took ship for Aden, promising the people that we would come again.

"On Wednesday, April 8th, we reached Baroum, a village of palms, bananas, and cotton plantations, with about eighty houses and a living well of excellent water, from which the ships are supplied. There was not a single Koran in the place, and the people are very simple-minded. We planted a number of Scriptures there and set sail at midnight.

"On Thursday, the 9th, we spoke to the sailors, as was our custom in every vessel in which we sailed, about salvation and other religious subjects. They disputed warmly and we answered them from the Koran. They were amazed at our knowing the Koran, and were

ADEN BAZAARS, WHERE KAMIL PREACHED.

at once convinced by the proofs we brought from it. We planted a Bible among them and every day we spoke with them until they began to love us and said, 'We can only yield assent to everything you say.' We prayed always so that they could hear and understand.

"At length, on Saturday, April 11th, we

reached Aden in peace and found our brother, Mr. Cantine, in health. We congratulated each other on our safety. Mr. Cantine is soon going to Muscat, and we told him of the various incidents of our blessed journey, and he greatly rejoiced at the door which God had opened to us for the entrance of his word. During the day our brother, Ibrahim, called with Mr. Rasheed and read a chapter from the Bible, and we offered thanksgiving to God for his providence over us in this journey. The next day I called on my Moslem friend and found a number of Arabs with him, and we talked of our journey and of the religion of Christ. He is of liberal views and many young men visit him, seeking after the true faith. May his house become a little church and spread to every part of Aden."

(Conclusion of the journal.)

"We offer our thanks and praise to our heavenly Father, and to the Son of his love, and to his Holy Spirit, to each of whom it becomes us to offer our reverence and worship, now and evermore, for going with us to carry his word to those who had never before known the true knowledge. And we ask of his divine Majesty that he will attend us and help us in all our future journeys to which he shall separate us for the spread of his word. Yes, we know of a truth that he—be he praised and exalted!—if he begins a work will perfect it, especially in the spread of his word in all parts of the world. Amen.

"*Note.*—The district which we visited has only one great castle and most of the places have few houses.

"From Mejrud, the limit of British jurisdiction, to Makullah, in the wilds there is no safety for travelers except by paying money to each sultan to take you through his territory to the next, and so on. From Belhaf to Makullah there is less danger. From Makullah to the east it is remarkably safe.

"But the best and the sweetest and the most delicious of all the glad tidings which we have written is this: We have planted in the Lord's vineyard, in this blessed journey, one hundred and ten copies of the Arabic Scriptures. Eight remained over, which I have sold in Aden. We pray the Lord of the vineyard that he will cause these plants to grow and bring great benefit and good fruits to the honor of our compassionate Redeemer, the Lord Jesus Christ. Amen.

"The penitent youth who confesses his sins,
        "KAMIL ABDUL MESSIAH."

ARAB TRAVELERS.

Kamil's affection for his father led him to pray earnestly that he, too, might be brought to the Christian faith and the joys of the gospel, and on the 28th of the month Shaaban, 1308, A. H., the Mohammedan date, or March 26, 1891, he wrote a letter to his father, sending me a copy, of which the following is a literal translation:

"ADEN, ARABIA, 28th Shaaban, 1308, A. H.,
"or March 26, 1891, A. D.

" Praise to God alone.

" To his excellency, his lordship, my revered father, the Hajj Muhy ed Deen Effendi, the most honored: may the Lord prolong his continuance. Amen.

"After kissing your dear hands with all reverence and respect and asking your continued prayers in my behalf, I would state to your lordship that—praise and thanks to God—I reached Port Said in good health and remained there twenty days, awaiting a cheap steamer. I then took passage and reached Aden safely. It is true that your son had some trials and suffering at sea, but the Lord (may his name be praised!) preserved me in his providence through his favor and his grace, and I met my friends, the honored missionaries, to whom I was journeying. Their work is preaching the Christian religion, that is, proclaiming to Mohammedans the glad tidings of salvation in Jesus Christ (Aiesa, the Son of Mary).

"I teach them Arabic and they teach me the Tourah and the Injeel [Old and New Testaments] and a little English, and I help them in their work of preaching, which is my chief aim and object. For this thing I came to Aden, the land of the Arabs, for I am bound even more than foreign missionaries to teach and preach the gospel of salvation to the children of my own race.

"You know, dear father, that I had neglected all religion and cared nothing about it. I gave no thought to this life nor to the resurrection and devoted none of my time to the worship of God, but was wandering in the sea of evil, engrossed with the world and its pleasures.

"My conscience reproved me for my sins, and I felt conscious that a heavy burden of sin was accumulating upon me. At length came the time of my repentance. I asked God to have mercy upon me and help me to overcome the lusts of the soul and the body, to forgive me all my sins, to cleanse my heart and preserve it from the temptations of the evil one, the devil. I asked all this of God with fervent prayer and mighty perseverance. And he looked upon me (may he be praised and exalted!) with the eye of pity, love, and joy. He had compassion on my youth and my life, for he is wont to treat his penitent children with tenderness and love. Especially does he love and rejoice and delight in the penitence of young men who forsake their fleshly lusts. He has expressed this in his own precious words, 'There is joy in heaven over one sinner that repenteth, more than over ninety and nine just persons, which need no repentance.' Oh, my dear father, I am sure that God has forgiven me and pardoned my transgressions. He has sought me to become one of his children and a laborer in his vineyard; yes, one of those who has received his favor and whom he has forgiven. God has sent to me his pure Spirit to teach me and preserve me from my foes, the flesh, the world, and the devil. He has conferred freely upon me a new garment and taken off the old garment with its works. Thanks to his exalted and most holy Majesty for this love and tender compassion. May his holy name be blessed forever and ever! Amen.

"I will hereafter inform your lordship about my work in Aden, and of the regeneration wrought in me with more of details. Rejoice, yes I say rejoice, over your son Kamil, for God has received him and pardoned him and hears his prayers. He has attended him in all his journey and never forsaken him. God forbid that he should leave me or forsake me after I have known him and become one of his own children and disciples. He is always at my right hand teaching me, guiding me to his commandments, to hear his word, and keeping me from violating his precepts. Oh, my honored and precious father, your former son Kamil has died with all his works, and now you have a new son Kamil, accepted with God, who attends him all night long and throughout the day.

"My work is study, reading, teaching, and preaching to my brethren, the Mohammedans. May God enlighten their hearts and send his Holy Spirit to illumine their minds, that they may know God with a true knowledge, and distinguish between the true and false prophets. Amen and Amen.

"My salutations to all my brethren. As I have told you of my work in Aden, I wish to ask you four questions:

"I. Is it lawful for your son to read the Old and the New Testaments?

"II. If not, why not?

"III. Are the Old and New Testaments books of God?

"IV. Were they written by inspiration of God sent upon his honored apostles?

"I would request that your lordship will honor me with an answer to these four questions, that the thoughts of your son may be at rest concerning them, and I will be greatly obliged to you.

"I close my letter by kissing your pure hands and asking your good prayers, my honored father.

"May I not be bereaved of you. Amen. And may you live forever.

"Your obedient son confessing his sins,

"KAMIL."

To this letter his father sent the following reply:

"BEIRUT, 24th Ramadan, 1308, A. H.
"April 20, 1891.
"Praise to God alone.

"To his excellency, our beloved and honored son, the Sayyid Kamil Effendi Aietany, the respected: may his continuance be prolonged. Amen.

"After sending you abundant salutations and the mercy of God and his blessings, and kissing your cheeks with all longing and affection, we hope to see you soon in the best of health.

"After this we say that, while we were looking for good news from you, your precious letter of

28th Shaaban arrived. We read it rejoicing at your safe arrival. We had been in great anxiety owing to the long delay of your letter, and were not relieved until it came, assuring us—praise to God!—of your health and prosperity. And we gave thanks to God for this. May he be exalted!

"You inform me that you have repented to-

BEDAWIN AND CAMELS.

ward God and avoided what he forbids and given up doing what displeases him, and that you are earnestly trying to act according to his pure law, devoted to his worship. Be he exalted, as he pleases!

"We were greatly rejoiced at what God has conferred upon you.

"I enjoin you (the favor of God be with you)

to persevere in his worship (be he exalted!) and do not neglect to mention * him always, for by mention of him the heart is assured, and it is imperishable gain.

"Persevere in the five hours of prayer daily with prayer for his honored Prophet our Lord and Mediator Mohammed, upon him be prayer and peace.

"Continue to read the precious Koran, and may you suffer no sloth nor weariness in the worship of God. This is the only way to insure God's favor toward us. We ask of him, exalted, to confirm us and you in his own true religion and his right way, by his grace and favor. Amen.

"With regard to your questions, I reply: 'Follow the divine word in his precious book, the Koran: "What the apostle has bidden, accept, what he has forbidden, reject."' This verse from the Koran means that we should obey the command of our Prophet Mohammed, (on him be prayer and peace!) and refrain from what he has forbidden.

"Now as to his commands, he has bidden us to worship God, exalted, according to the religion God has given, especially to our Prophet

---

* The sheikh evidently means by "mention" of God, the zikr or the tasbih.

Mohammed (on him be prayer and peace!) according to the word of the precious Koran. That is the religion of Islam.

"The only true creed is this, 'I testify that there is no god but God, and Mohammed is his Apostle.'

"Then the five daily prayers, then alms. If one has seven hundred piasters [$25] he is rich and must give alms, and if he has more he must give accordingly. He must perform the pilgrimage to the house of God, the Haram in Mecca if he is able. One visit is enough to pay the obligation. He must also fast during the month of Ramadan. Any one who neglects any of these duties is not a perfect Moslem, and all his worship is corrupt.

"As to what is forbidden by Mohammed, our lord (on him be prayer and peace!):

"He forbids our joining anything with God in worship and bids us leave all other religions and follow his religion which God has enjoined, and obey its injunctions. These things are a duty and we must follow them. He has forbidden us from following another religion.

"Now with regard to your four questions, we reply:

"I. It is lawful to read the Old and New Testaments, but unlawful to act according to them, because the book of the Great God which he sent down to our lord Mohammed (on him be prayer and peace!) has abrogated the wisdom of all previous laws.

"II. This is already answered in the above.

"III. The Old and New Testaments are the books of God. He sent down the Old Testament [Tourah] to our lord Moses the Kaleem [the addressed] of God, on him be the prayers of God! and the New Testament [Injeel] he sent down to our Lord Aiesa [Jesus], on him be peace!

"IV. The Old and New Testaments were sent down to the honored apostles by inspiration from God.

"We have now told you what is necessary in reply to your questions, and may the Lord open to you the truth and may you live forever.

"It is true that we believe that God, exalted, sent down the Tourah to our lord Moses and the Injeel to our Lord Aiesa, but the laws of the Koran have abrogated the laws of the Tourah and the Injeel, therefore it is not lawful to accept their teachings unless they conform to what is in his book, as for instance, the ten commandments, 'Thou shalt not commit adultery,' etc.

"Such things as the following: that Lot (on him be peace!) drank wine and committed adultery with his daughters; that David committed adultery; that Solomon in his old age worshiped idols—these things we do not believe at all.

"Nor do we believe in the Trinity, for 'God is the only One God, he has no wife or Son.' All the texts prove that he is One. He said (be he exalted!): 'If there be other gods than God, they are corrupt.'

"Now, since the Old and New Testaments contain statements of this kind, it must appear to you, my darling son, apple of my eye, that they are perverted and corrupted, and that they are not the Old and New Testaments which were sent down to Moses and Jesus, upon whom be peace! It is not lawful for you to read them for any other object than for the defense of your own religion. But to preach from them and to summon the servants of God to believe in their falsehoods, this is one of the greatest crimes, and he who does it, if he is not an infidel is worse than an infidel, and his torment hereafter will be greater. I therefore warn you, my son, from this vain business which will take you to hell. What is the world but a deceitful possession? If you trust in it it will lead you to the brink of the pit. If you do not give good heed, O apple of my eye, you will plunge into the pit and be among those that perish, which may God forbid. I counsel you, my son Kamil, to return to your country and not distress my thoughts and leave me to die of longing for you. Take the advice of your father and upon you be peace and the mercy and blessing of God.

"Your father,

"M—— A——."

This reply of Kamil's father takes up only one of the Mohammedan arguments against the Old and New Testaments, viz., that they have been abrogated by the Koran. They also claim that the Bible has been changed and corrupted so as to prove the divinity of Christ and his death and resurrection. The admixture of paternal tenderness with religious warning is very touching. Once when Kamil was in Mount Lebanon his father wrote him that if he apostatized from Islam he might be obliged to take his life. This was probably meant for intimidation, but it is quite in harmony with the universal opinion of Moslems that apostasy is a forfeiture of wife and children and property and life.

Kamil replied to his father as follows:

"ADEN, 13 Zil Kaadeh, 1308, A. H.

"June 19, 1891.

"To his excellency, the good and revered my lord and father, the most honored, the

East African Arabs and Native Hut.

Sheikh M. Effendi . . . . . the most exalted, may his life continue. Amen.

"After kissing your pure hands and asking your good prayers, and inquiring after your noble and precious pleasure, I would state to your lordship that in an hour which is the ornament of the hours, and which will be mentioned with joy in all time, I was honored by the receipt of the answer of your lordship, dated 24th Ramadan, 1308, to the four questions previously presented by your son. The purport of your reply is that the reading of the Old and New Testaments is lawful, but to act in accordance with their teaching is wrong, inasmuch as the great book of God which he sent down to our lord Mohammed (on whom be prayer and peace from God!) has abrogated the wisdom of all other laws; also that the Tourah and Injeel are books of God, the Tourah being sent down to our lord Moses the Kaleem [speaker] of God (may the prayers of God be upon him!) and the Injeel upon our Lord Aiesa [Jesus], upon him be peace. Also that they were sent down to the honored apostles by inspiration from God. You also say that it is unlawful to receive what is in them unless it be in accordance with our book, as the ten commandments. But such statements as that the prophets like Lot and David and Solomon sinned against God, we can not believe at all. Nor do we believe in the Trinity because there is the one only God who has no wife nor Son, and there are many texts to prove that he is One. You also say that as the Old and New Testaments contain such things, it is plain that they have been changed and corrupted, and that they are not the Old and New Testaments sent down to Moses and Jesus (on them be peace!), and that we should not read them for any other object than the defense of our religion; and to preach from them and call God's servants to believe in their falsehoods, is the greatest of crimes, and whosoever does it, if he be not an infidel is worse than the infidels. You warn me against this and advise me to return home in peace. You also enjoin me to please God and continue in his worship and direct me to observe the rites and observances such as prayer and fasting, alms, etc., and to continue reading the precious Koran, and so on to the end.

"On reading this letter of your lordship I overflowed with the offering of the greatest reverence and hearty thanksgivings to your fatherly tenderness, in the joy and great gladness you show at God's grace to me in giving me repentance and forgiveness out of his favor and love. And what increased my joy is your excellency's congratulations to me for this great divine gift to me. I thank God for his surpassing kindness and his great favor. I supplicate his exalted and glorious Majesty that he may confirm me in the sound faith and the true religion, that I may continue in his worship according to his will and pleasure. I hope that he will preserve me from the wiles of the devil and his evil ways, and preserve you in his providence by his favor and his goodness. Amen.

"After this, your excellency my father, I began to examine and investigate all the contents of your honorable letter, seeking rest for my mind, but the result was that my mind became more disturbed than ever before, and this after I had read it over a second and third time.

"Therefore, after asking your permission and requesting your favor and your fatherly prayers, I would say in reply to your excellency:

"We read in the Koran, Sura 8, v. 8, as follows:

"'That he might prove his truth to be the truth, and bring to naught that which is naught though the impious were averse to it.'

"Now, as to the statement of your lordship that 'it is lawful to read the Old and New Testaments,' how excellent and how fine is your reply, did it end there. But you then say, 'It is wrong to act according to them.' This makes our condition like that of a man who makes a great feast of good things, providing the most luscious fruits, the finest vegetables, the rarest of fowls and fishes, the purest of meats and the richest buklawah, sweet pastry, etc., and when the invited guests had all assembled and were seated around the table inhaling the delicious odors, looking upon the tempting viands, and just taking up the spoons to eat, the master of the house should rise and say aloud, 'Divide not a single loaf, partake of not a single dish, and eat nothing of the sweets.' What an hour of wretchedness would it be to those invited guests. They would sit amazed. Woe to them! How can they refrain from the expected pleasure? Woe to them if they violate propriety and eat!

"Oh my dear father, such would be my state, the state of the guests, and yours that of the master of the house. For since you say it is lawful to read the books, I opened them and read the following precious treasures: Christ said, 'Whatsoever ye will that men should do unto you, do ye also likewise unto them, for this is the law and the prophets.' He also said, 'Come unto me, all ye that labor and are heavy laden, and I will give you rest.' 'I am the resurrection, and the life; he that believeth in me, though he were dead, yet shall he live; and whosoever liveth and believeth in me shall never die.' He also said, 'I am the vine, ye are the branches; he that abideth in me, and I in him, the same bringeth forth much fruit: for without me ye can do nothing.' 'Fear not: for I have redeemed thee, I have called thee by thy name; thou art mine. When thou passest through the waters, I will be with thee; and through the rivers, they shall not overflow thee; when thou walkest through the fire, thou shalt not be burned; neither shall the flame kindle upon thee. For I am the Lord thy God, the Holy One of Israel, thy Saviour.' 'I will never leave thee nor forsake thee.' Then I read this command of Christ,' Thou shalt love the Lord thy God with all thy heart, and with all thy soul, and with all thy mind; and thy neighbor as thyself.' And God says in Isaiah: 'Though your sins be as scarlet, they shall be as white as snow; though they be red like crimson, they shall be as wool.' And so it is, my honored father, from the beginning of the Old Testament to the end of the New; I find verses like these which delight and refresh and quicken the heart and soften it; and when I wish to appropriate them with all my heart, and believe them, on account of the delight I have in reading them, then you call out to me, 'Break not a loaf, touch not a dish' ('it is wrong to act according to them'), and I become like those poor invited guests, or rather I become like the man of whom Christ said, 'he built his house on the sand, and the wind and the storms came and destroyed it,' or like the donkey mentioned in the Koran, 'like a donkey laden with books.' And I think you would not consent to my being like a donkey carrying books.

"And, more than this, we see that we poor sinners with all the weakness of our intellects and the defects of our understanding, do nothing and write nothing without an object. Our object is to effect something by what we do or write. Now how is it with God, be he praised and exalted? Infallible in respect to sin or forgetfulness; would he command these books to be written without any object? God forbid! God forbid!

"The divine inspiration of these books, then, must have been for some great object, and that, the keeping of their commandments and avoidance of what they forbid, also the knowledge of the truth in the inward parts and that one may distinguish between the true and false prophets, and worship God spiritually, for God is a Spirit: and they that worship him must worship him in spirit and in truth.

"The inference then, is plain—if reading these books is lawful, obedience to them is necessary. As one has said, 'The carelessness of the heart about truth is one of the greatest faults.'

"Now, as to the Koran having abrogated all previous laws, my dear father, I cannot find in the Koran a single verse showing that it has abrogated the Old and New Testaments, but the contrary. It says in the Surat el Anaam, 'We gave Moses the book complete as to whatever is excellent and an explanation of every matter and a direction and a mercy, if haply they might believe in the meeting of their Lord.' Then in Surat Hood, 'And before him is the book of Moses a guide and a mercy. These have faith in it, but the partisans who believe not in it are menaced with the fire. Have thou no doubts about that book, for it is the very truth from thy Lord, but most men will not believe.' And in Surat el Kosos : 'And verily we gave Moses the book after that we had destroyed the former generations, an enlightenment unto mankind and a direction and a mercy, if haply they might be admonished.' Also in Surat el Maledat : 'And we caused Jesus, the Son of Mary, to follow in their footsteps, attesting the Scripture of the Tourah which preceded him : and we gave him the Gospel wherein is guidance and light, which attests the Tourah that preceded it, and a direction and an admonition to the pious.'

"There are many passages of like meaning, but for want of time we will let these suffice. 'The wise is satisfied with a little.' It is clear to me, your excellency, my father, from the meaning of the preceding passages, that the Old and New Testaments are complete and perfect in everything needed in religion: a guidance to mercy, an enlightenment to all men of all sects and faiths, lights to their hearts, by which they see truth and discriminate between truth and falsehood, and a guide to the laws which are the true way of God, and a mercy, for if we act according to them we will receive mercy from God, be his name praised and exalted!

"Now, is there higher praise than this? What book has been described and characterized with such beautiful epithets?

"Further, it is plain from the above verses from the Koran that they who disbelieve the words of God shall have great torment; that God is exalted, a God of vengeance, and the fire is their portion. Now, if we turn aside from the decisions of the Old and New Testaments and put in their places our own words and the words of other men, for the sake of maintaining our worldly glory, we are no doubt infidels and the fire is our portion. May God forbid!

"Now, after all these quotations and proofs you say, nay, you charge the Koran with saying that the wisdom of the Old and New Testaments is abrogated. How then shall I escape from the wrath of God at the day of resurrection, when neither parent nor children can profit us? Then will prove true the proverb, 'Every sheep is suspended by his own leg,' when I stand before the great bar of judgment. We would also add your own remark, 'They are books of God. He sent down the Tourah to Moses, his familiar speaker, and the Gospel to our Lord Jesus (upon them be peace!), and they were sent down with inspiration from God to the honored apostles.'

"Oh, my misfortune; Oh, the misfortune of others if we do not read it with awe and reverence, with obedience and respect.

"Then, as to the declaration of your lordship, 'We have no right to accept any of their teachings unless they accord with our own book, *e.g.*, as the ten commandments,' you have in this word dragged down the Bible to the level of a moral or a story-book, since, according to your claim, if there be anything in harmony with our own selves and our own lusts, and within our comprehension, we will yield to it and believe it, otherwise we will let it go.

"This is not proper treatment of the book of God. We ought to hear what it says with all reverence and attention, and believe all it says from its word, 'In the beginning God created the heaven and the earth,' to its last word, 'Amen'; for 'all Scripture is given by inspiration of God, and is profitable for doctrine, for reproof, for correction, for instruction in righteousness; that the man of God may be perfect, thoroughly furnished unto every good work.'

"Let us see what the Koran says on this point, and also the words of Baidhawi, the learned commentator. Surat en Nissa: 'Oh, ye that believe, believe in God and in his prophet, and in the book which he hath revealed to his prophet, and in the book which he revealed from before.' Now hear the Moslem commentator, Baidhawi. 'The Moslems are here addressed, or the hypocrites, or the believers from among the people of the book, according to the following tradition: Ibn Sallam and his companions said, "O prophet of God, we believe in thee and in thy book, and in Moses and in the Tourah and Ezra, and we disbelieve in all besides." Then was this text revealed, "Believe," etc., as above.' Baidhawi then says, 'That is, be steadfast in the faith thereof and perpetually rest thereupon, and believe in it with all your hearts as ye believe in it with your lips; or believe with a comprehensive faith which shall embrace all the Scriptures and apostles; for the faith of a part is as no faith at all, and whosoever disbelieveth in them or in any part thereof has wandered from the truth into wide and dangerous error, and can hardly return to it.'

"Now, after all this, how can I believe in a part and deny the rest, and thus become a wanderer 'into wide and dangerous error,' far from the way of truth so that I can hardly return to it? I would thus become a fool or a 'hypocrite,' which may God forbid. No; I will read them and believe them with all my heart, with all longing and zeal, unless you will give me proofs to the contrary, strong proofs from the word of God, not from the words of men; but this you are far from able to do. You would far better unite with me in reading them and thus be of those who are good.

"Now as to the evidence and proof of your assertion that the Tourah and the Injeel have been changed and are not the very Tourah and Injeel sent down to our lord, Moses, the speaker with God, and to our Lord Aiesa, the Christ (upon them be peace!), for the reason that, as you say, they impute sin to the prophets, we reply as follows: You say that the Bible charges Lot and David with adultery, and Solomon in his old age with idolatry. But this does not prove to me that the Scriptures have been changed. We read in the Koran that David took his brother's ewe lamb (Sura 2), and Adam ate of the forbidden tree (Sura 2), and Abraham was an idolater, and Joseph longed for the Egyptian woman, and that Mohammed was in error and received guidance and that he was wroth with a blind man, and that Aaron worshiped the calf when his brother was on the mountain.

"We find many such cases in the Koran, and it is not at all unlikely that the rest of the prophets also sinned against the law of the Lord. They were men like ourselves, and acted as we act, for by nature they were inclined toward sin in carnal matters. We confess, indeed, and declare that the prophets were infallibly preserved in their prophecies and in writing that for which they were inspired by God (be he praised and exalted!), but in other respects they were like us in everything.

"This very fact has given me new vigor and strength and faith in reading the Scriptures, and has proved to me that they are not changed, for it makes no distinction, but declares all to be sinners in the eyes of God. All need forgiveness and to ask pardon of the high and lofty God. And, further, we should not reject anything in God's word, because it is above the comprehension of our intellects, but yield acquiescence and believe it, whatever it may be.

"No proof has yet been offered of any change in the old books of the Old and New Testaments. They are before the whole world. Where is the proof of any vital change? Hundreds and thousands of copies and translations are spread out before the world. Now, my dear father, let us who maintain and insist that the Old and New Testaments have been perverted and changed examine the matter for ourselves. Let us go to the very bottom of the question. Let us print our investigations and publish them to the world. Christians have no fear of minute inquiry, and it may even be that they would pay us for our labors; for they are constantly expending money to search into everything pertaining to the Bible. No, my father; even as it is certain that no proof has been found of a vital change in the Bible, neither will one be found in the future.

"One of the insuperable difficulties in the way of changing and tampering with the text of the Bible is the multitude of versions and translations, and their wide distribution over the earth. To gather them all and change them all in the same way so that they would all agree in all the different languages would be simply impossible. If a few were changed, the rest would remain pure as a proof of the change, and thus the fraud would easily be detected. Another difficulty in the way of changing the Old Testament is the excessive care taken by the Jews to guard the purity of the Hebrew text. They counted the very letters in the Pentateuch and could tell the middle letter, and also the middle sentence, word and letter, in the rest of the Old Testament. They know how many times each letter of the alphabet occurs in the whole book. For instance, they found that the letter Aleph occurs 42,377 times, and Beth 32,318 times, etc. This grew out of their extraordinary care of the text, and a change in the language while in their hands was utterly impossible.

"And more than all this, the bitter hostility between the Jews and Christians would make any collusion to change the text out of the question. Had a Jew dared to change it, the Christian would have risen up and forbidden him, given him the lie and cursed him, and the same would happen did the Christian change it.

"And, finally, I would say that if a man came to your excellency and said, 'A large part of the Koran has been changed and perverted,' you would answer him instantly, ' Be silent, you infidel ; the words inspired of God are not subject to change, nor would any one dare to exscind or pervert them.'

"And so I can say that the Tourah and Injeel are the books of God, and no one would dare to stretch out his hand with evil intent against them, after reading the warning in the last chapter of the noble gospel which says, ' If any man shall take away from the words of the book of this prophecy, God shall take away his part out of the book of life, and from the things which are written in this book.'

" I think that the above is enough to convince you that the Old and New Testaments are the very books given by inspiration ' to Moses and to our Lord Jesus Christ.' God grant that this may satisfy your excellency and remove the false suspicion and impression with regard to God's word. I hope you will read them with joy and gladness and believe in all they contain, and thus join the goodly company of those who attain the favor of God—be he praised and exalted ! ☉ Lord enlighten the mind of my father and of all the Mohammedans. Amen.

"And now as to your claim that the preaching of the gospel and calling men to believe in the Scriptures is wrong, as you urge, and that it is ' the greatest of crimes, and he who does it, if he be not an infidel, is worse than an infidel,' etc., I would say, my honored father, that after the convincing proofs I have given you of the authenticity of the Old and New Testaments, the impossibility of their having been corrupted and changed, and that they are the very books ' sent down ' to our lord Moses and to our Lord Jesus Christ, I read these books and preach them, and teach all that they contain, and invite my Moslem brethren to believe in them. I believe in all they say in word, deed, and thought. And I also invite your excellency and my brethren and my kindred and my friends to believe in these two noble books. Oh, my joy, my delight, would you but read them and believe what they contain of treasures and precious jewels! I entreat you to read them if it be but once, and you would then see how your heart would cling to them. Then would you exclaim, 'Yes, there is no doubt nor question about their being the books of God!' And every day, yea, every hour you would read them with joy and teach and preach and guide others to these precious jewels. Then you would say, ' My son Kamil is right; the truth is with him, and he has attained the favor of God—be he praised and exalted!'

"Again, you charge me to repeat constantly the name of God, Allah. Oh, my revered father, God himself has charged me not to take his name in vain, in the streets and lanes, in the outhouses and vile places, but he commands me to mention his name in the place of worship, and there to ask of his Majesty all things, and not to use his name in vain repetitions, without meaning and without cause. Supposing a man loved another whose name is Ahmed, and then went around the streets and lanes and unclean places, saying Ahmed, Ahmed, Ahmed, Ahmed, Ahmed, Ahmed, etc., a thousand times, you may be sure that Ahmed would prosecute him at law and imprison him for having ridiculed him and disgraced his name. How then is it with the name of God? (Be he praised and exalted!) Alas, alas, for this evil habit, in use among the Moslems alone. A Moslem will walk along the road saying 'Allah, Allah, Allah, Allah, there is no God but Allah, there is no God but Allah,' and this a thousand times a day or more. Now, since your excellency has enjoined me to obey the ten commandments, I have given up this wretched practice of repeating the name of God on all occasions and in improper places, for the third commandment says, 'Thou shalt not take the name of the Lord thy God in vain; for the Lord will not hold him guiltless that taketh his name in vain.'

"With regard to prayer, do not feel anxiety on my account. I will not neglect prayer and supplication to God (be he praised and exalted!). At morning and evening and noon, when I awake, and before I eat or sleep, I will not forget to offer prayer to his exalted and glorious Majesty, asking forgiveness and help in our work of preaching and all our labors. We offer thanksgiving for all the mercies he grants us from day to day. Yes, my father; my motto is, 'All things by prayer in spirit and in truth.'

"Then as to your expression 'Mohammed our Lord,' I can not find a single verse in the Koran which calls Mohammed (Sayyid) lord ; but he is a servant, one of the servants of God, as we all are his servants.

"As to Mohammed being our intercessor, I find many passages in the Koran which oppose this view. Sura 33 : 17. 'Who is he that will screen you from God, whether he choose to bring evil on you or to show you mercy ?' Sura 49 : 81. 'If thou ask forgiveness for them seventy times, God will by no means forgive them.' Sura 20 : 108. 'No intercession shall avail on that day save his whom the Merciful shall allow, and whose words he shall approve.' Sura 39 : 45. 'Intercession is wholly with God' ; and many others like these. We have it here clearly indicated that Mohammed did not regard himself as an agent or mediator or intercessor for mankind or for God's people, and, this being the case, would I not be regarded as foolish to ask his intercession, nay, more, as silly and perverse ?

"You also ask me to read the Koran continually. Do not feel anxious on this point. I am constantly reading it and trying to understand its meaning, and to find out which parts are abrogated (mansukh) and which verses abrogate others (nasikh). Every day I find strange things in it which I had not thought of, and which probably have never occurred to you or to my brethren the Mussulmans. May the Lord enlighten their hearts and teach them the truth more and more. Amen.

"As to giving alms, this I do in secret and, as the gospel says : ' God which seeth in secret shall reward ' me ' openly.' ' But when thou doest alms, let not thy left hand know what thy right hand doeth : that thine alms may be in secret : and thy Father which seeth in secret himself shall reward thee openly.'

"As to fasting, it is necessary in times of special need. As to pilgrimage to Beit Allah el Haram in Mecca, I am not just now able to make that journey.

"As to your injunction that we join no one with God as an object of worship, I have learned from the first and second commandments not to do so. God forbid that I should worship anything besides God. God forbid that I should say that ' God is but one of three gods.' There is no god but the one God, and he who joins any person or thing with God is an infidel. God forbid that I should be an infidel ; that I should join any other object of worship with God the Creator of the heavens and the earth by the word of his power, and to whom alone we should offer worship and adoration now and for evermore.

"Now, as to the question of the Trinity, we would better leave it for the present, as you can not understand this mystery while in a state of prejudice. When you accept the truth of the Old and New Testaments, you will easily comprehend this mystery. It is above our intellects. Our not being able to understand it does not make it impossible or contrary to reason and a sound mind, nor make it right for us to reject it. By no means; for God has not been pleased to reveal to us his secret things. If we have a right to reject it because we can not comprehend it, we should have a right to reject other things which God has revealed which are beyond our comprehension, as, for instance, the day of judgment and final account, God's self-existence, his eternity, his being uncaused and the Cause of all causes, his omnipresence everywhere at one and the same time, his omniscience, his creating the heavens and the earth by the word of his power, and many other truths like these.

"The mystery of the Trinity is not greater than other mysteries of God—be he exalted! God has a right to reveal to us a truth without giving special reasons or particulars, and we are bound to receive such truth from him in humility and hearty faith, and we should receive the doctrine of the Trinity as we receive that of the Unity, without attempting to explain particularly its mode. I know that your excellency finds this point very difficult ; but when your heart has been illumined with divine light, you will understand this at once and readily. Do not say, ' My son Kamil has become an infidel.' God forbid ! But say, ' He knows the truth far more than before.'

"You counsel me to return to my native country. This is not possible at present, for I am busy in the vineyard of the Lord, sowing his word among the people of Ishmael, even my brethren the Moslems. But, if the Lord will, I will return after a few years to see you and kiss your hands with all filial reverence.

"This is what I wish to lay before your excellency, trusting that in your fatherly kindness you will not regard my letters as presumption in your child, but will treat me with your well-known courtesy and goodness.

"In order to attain a knowledge of the truth we must investigate with great precision, and this precision must be the greater as the subject is greater which we examine. There is no subject which concerns us in this transient life more than religion, on which hang our happiness and everlasting life. We are bound to search and examine as to the true way which leads to God —be he praised and exalted!

SOUTHERN ARABIA RELIGIOUS SHEIKH.

"If, then, there are conclusive and convincing proofs in refutation of the arguments presented by your obedient son, I am ready to give heed to them and to submit to them. I am seeking to know the true way which leads to salvation from the wrath of God; only this, and not merely to establish my own views. My only object is to worship God in truth lest I perish forever, which may God forbid!

"Yes, my revered father, I am obedient to you in everything but religion (this belongs to God) unless you prove to me that your religion is true.

"I now close my letter by kissing your pure hands and asking your good prayers, my lord and father; may I not be bereaved of you.

"Your obedient son,

"KAMIL."

To this letter the father sent a reply, evidently written by one of the learned Moslem sheikhs, full of venomous bitterness, attacking the Scriptures, and using the well-known arguments of the satanic book known as "Izhar el Hoc." The father is made to curse Kamil and consign him to hell as an apostate.

On September 15, 1891, Kamil wrote me as follows:

..... After the usual preface: "After kissing your pure hands and asking for your good prayers, I beg to inclose a letter received from his excellency, my father, in answer to my last letter to him. And, Oh, my dear Doctor, when I received this letter I was ill, and when I read it I was filled with grief and deep regret, and at three o'clock my fever increased greatly with severe chills, and all on account of what it stated as to the overwhelming grief and suffering of my aged father on reading my last letter. I had hoped to rejoice his heart by that letter and to lead him to give up his old errors, and my chief object was his salvation and his coming into the fold of our Saviour—to him be glory and honor forever! But he is angry with me and denounces me with the title of infidel and other abusive epithets, such as I had never heard in all my life. And he omits all the endearing names and words which a loving father uses to a son. You will see all this on reading the letter, and I know that your tears will flow with mine over the great sorrow which has befallen your son Kamil.

"Alas! what can I do to please my dear father? For while on one hand I am bound to obey and honor him and go to him and comfort him, yet this is impossible now, as I am busy in the vineyard of the Lord, who is greater than all. I can not leave my blessed, holy, joyous work to which the Lord Jesus Christ, Lord of the vineyard, has set me apart. Oh, my perplexity and my sorrow! Oh, thou merciful and everlasting God, help me, comfort me, look upon me, compassionate me! Oh, my Saviour, be gracious to thy disciple, thy soldier, Kamil!

"I beg you, dear sir, to write me at once and comfort me with words from your own mouth. Even as my father according to the flesh has grieved me as to my earthly life, so comfort and rejoice my heart as to my spiritual and everlasting life. I have good hope in the Lord Jesus Christ, my Saviour, that he will regard my condition and guide me to what he loves and approves, and neither leave nor forsake me, as he has promised.

"In the letter above referred to, the writer claims that the Christian Old and New Testaments are not the ones referred to in the Koran, but have been perverted and tampered with to suit Christian teachings. I do not feel able just now to answer this line of argument, as I have not access to the authorities he refers to, but hope to do so in the future. Please read the letter and return it to me.

"Here it is fitting that I express my hearty thanks to his excellency, my beloved brother, Rev. Mr. Zwemer, who, during my illness with fever, came at once and visited me constantly, giving me medicine, comforting me, and praying for me on my bed. He certainly did everything in his power in favor and kindness. By the doctor's orders I went down to the port city of Aden for a few days for a change of air. But my trust is in the great and only Physician. Praise and thanks to God, I have now regained my health.

"To-morrow, I expect to make a voyage to Jabuti and Obock, on the African coast, with a Scripture bookseller named Istefanus Mukkar, a most zealous youth in the sale of God's word. After our return I hope to write you of our journey, if the Lord spares my life.

"I have recently been reading the Arabic D'Aubigné's 'History of the Reformation,' in order to understand the history of the early church. I am now reading with Mr. Zwemer Woodbridge's 'Theology,' in English, which was sent me as a gift from America. After studying the subject in English, I at once go over the same theme in Dr. Dennis's 'Arabic Theology.'

"The Rev. Mr. —— has sent me from America two English books on preaching, by Mr. Spurgeon. I thank all these friends for their kind gifts of books to one whom they have never seen.

"Perhaps you would like to hear news about Sana (the capital of Arabia Felix). The Bedawin Arabs have neither first nor last. They are like the locusts. Every day a thousand or five hundred arrive to join them. They have four thousand muskets. The Turks charge the English with supplying them with arms. The natives of Hadeideh send them arms and ammunition secretly. The Turks had two thousand troops and now have four thousand. The Bedawin attacked Sana, fought the troops, and killed some of them and many of the wretched Jews. The Bedawin finally took three-quarters of the city and cut the telegraph and the roads to the coast. During this time the waly, Salim Pasha, died, but whether by poison or otherwise is not known. The new Turkish reinforcements from Syria and Constantinople are camped two days' journey from Sana and do not venture to advance. The new waly is three days west of Sana, and the Arabs have captured four hundred camels laden with military stores. The Italian consul here tells me that the war has continued two months and that multitudes of the Jews have emigrated to Jerusalem. It seems to me that God has stirred up the Bedawin to open the way for the entrance of his word and his disciples into Sana.

"The Turks are all Pharisees, but there is not a Nicodemus among them. This is the news from Sana. The Lord have pity on his servants there. Amen.

"I have much to say about God's word in Aden, but can not write more now. . . . .

"Since writing the above I have received yours of August 17th, and am cheered by its good news of my fellow-Moslem converts; and I rejoice to hear of the printing of the book, 'Sweet First Fruits.' May it prove a great means of leading our Mohammedan brethren to peace with God through Jesus Christ.

"I hope that Dr. Eddy and your daughter have had a safe voyage. The Lord preserve them and bring them back in peace.

"Word has come from our dear brother, Rev. Mr. Cantine, in Busrah, that he will soon return to us. May God bring him in safety with glad news of the entrance of the pure gospel into that land. It is probable that on his return I shall go with him and Mr. Zwemer to that region, taking a full supply of Arabic Scriptures. Please excuse the haste of this letter, as I am to journey to-morrow.

"Please extend the most fragrant salaams and sincere salutations to Mrs. Jessup and your children. The Lord preserve them and you in health. Do not fail to remember me in your prayers. Please salute for me Dr. Van Dyck, and Dr. Post, and Mr. Hardin. The Lord preserve them. Amen.

"Mr. Zwemer, Khawaja Ibrahim, and M.

Rasheed salute you. If you have any news of Mr. Van Tassel laboring among the Bedawin near Hums, please inform me. And also tell me of Mr. Richmond, who was studying Arabic in Mr. Hardin's school in Suk to go to Morocco.

"I now close by kissing your pure hands once and again, and may you continue in health.

"Yours, the penitent youth confessing his sins,
"KAMIL ABDUL MESSIAH."

THE VISIT TO OBOCK AND JABUTI.

"ADEN, October 14, 1891.

" . . . In my previous letter I told you of my father's letter and my expected visit to Obock and Jabuti with the colporteur of the British and Foreign Bible Society. We returned to-day from this blessed journey in the Lord's vineyard.

"Heeding our Lord's command, we sailed to Obock, where we remained but one day, as very few of the people speak Arabic, and there was no place to sleep or eat, but we planted one Bible there.

"We then went to Jabuti. This town is larger than Obock, and its people are more numerous and more courteous. They are chiefly Arabs, and simple-minded. The Lord opened the way for the preaching of his cross and sufferings there, and helped us. We hired a thatched house and remained eight days, planting seventy-three Bibles. I was greatly pleased with the visit. It will yet become a large place. Meat and fish are abundant and cheap, and its water is more delicious and sweet than all the water I have drunk during all my stay in Arabia. After this we returned to Aden, and I hope to send you the journal of the journey, as there is much that is encouraging in it, of our preaching in the name of our Saviour, the Lord Jesus Christ.

"The beloved Mr. Cantine sent to the zealous Mr. Zwemer to come to el Busrah, and he sailed for that place during my absence. The Lord preserve them, bring them back safely, and open the way for the entrance of his glorious gospel there. The news from our beloved brother Cantine, from Busrah, is very cheering as to the word of the Lord. I hope to tell you of it in detail in the future.

"I will write to my successors, the converts from Islam, in Lebanon. The Lord confirm them in faith, humility, and zeal, and all the Christian graces.

"According to the latest news the Turks have recaptured Sana, so I think the Lord does not will at present to open the way there for his gospel.

"On my return from Obock I found the inclosed letter from one of my Mohammedan disciples who called, and, not finding me, left this note. I was especially pleased with his signature, which is,

"'The learner in the Christian religion,

"'IBRAHIM ABDULLAH.'

". . . Mrs. Gardner is very useful in Sheikh Othman, as she can practice medicine among the women of the hareems.

"I hope soon to receive the 'Bakurah,' or 'Sweet First Fruits,' if it is published.

"Do not fail to remember me in your prayers in the family and in the church.

"KAMIL."

PROPOSED TRANSFER TO EL BUSRAH.

"ADEN, December 2, 1891."

After the usual salutations:

"I wish to inform you that the Rev. Mr. Zwemer has returned to Aden greatly pleased with el Busrah. He asked me whether I wished to go there. I replied 'Yes,' and if God wills, I shall sail for el Busrah in December, trusting in the gracious Lord, hoping that you will still pray for me as you have done, and I shall ever be most grateful.

"The Arab rebellion in Yemen is still moving

on foot and leg. After the occupation by the Turkish troops and all was quiet, suddenly the Arabs came down on the city by night, killed eight hundred troops, and disappeared.

"In my opinion the Turkish commander is right that it will take sixty thousand troops to end this war. Troops are constantly arriving. The Turkish mushir asked the Bedawin what they were fighting for. They replied, 'We want an Arab wali, Arab kadis, and immunity from taxes for five years, and after that we will pay one-half the tax previously levied.' The mushir answered, 'Lay down your arms and then we will discuss the matter.' They replied, 'We will never lay down our arms until you grant our demands.' If the Arabs hold out, there will be heavy fighting. The Lord have pity on his creatures.

"Please renew my subscription to your 'Neshra' journal, which I greatly value.

"My salutations to you all. The Lord preserve you by his providence. Amen.

"KAMIL ABDUL MESSIAH."

ARRIVAL IN EL BUSRAH.

Kamil sailed from Aden for Busrah December 10, 1891, on the S. S. "Chyebassa," and on his arrival wrote as follows :

"FROM EL BUSRAH TO OUR FLOWERY, BRIGHT BEIRUT.

"January 12, 1892.

"To Rev. H. H. Jessup, etc., etc.

"After kissing the tips of your fingers and asking for your righteous prayers and expressing my longing for you. I have now written you several letters and am anxiously awaiting your reply. I pray that the cause of the delay may be only good. Through your counsel and prayers I have now reached el Busrah, where, if God wills, I am to live in health and peace. As far as I can see, it will be a favorable place for our work in the Lord's vineyard. I am aware that, as you well know, there will be some little difficulty, as the government is in the hands of the Turks, but we know and believe that the power of God can overcome all power in heaven and earth. This hope will lead me to complete my work according to the will of God, hoping for the aid of your prayers.

"As it is the New Year, I say, with all reverence and joy, 'A Happy New Year to you and all your family. May you have many happy returns of the day in health and peace.' Please accept my congratulations and regard me always as one of your children. And may God spare your life.

"Your obedient son,

"KAMIL ABDUL MESSIAH."

In Busrah.

"From el Busrah to our Flowery, Bright Beirut.

"February 12, 1892.

"To Rev. H. H. Jessup, etc.: I was greatly distressed by the news of Mrs. Jessup's illness and pray earnestly that she may ere this have been fully restored to health. If you ask after my health, praise to God, I am well, and have begun to labor in this city of el Busrah, which the Lord of the vineyard has chosen for the entrance of the teaching of the cross.

"The Lord has opened the way for me for conversation with my brethren and sons of my country, the Moslems, for large numbers of them, as well as of the Christian sects, come to me by night and by day, and I speak to them of the glad tidings of salvation, as well and as wisely as I can, according as the Holy Spirit teaches me. Some have asked for Bibles and Testaments and we have supplied them, accompanying them with prayer to God that he will open their hearts to the knowledge of the truth, and lead them to read the Bible calmly and with propriety, seeking only the knowledge of the true religion in the Lord Jesus Christ. I hope you will not cease to help us by prayer for the good of my people.

"My father's letters have ceased coming after he wrote that letter which I sent you, so full of curses and abuses and wrath. The Lord guide him to the knowledge of the truth, and hasten the time of his coming into the fold of the beloved Jesus Christ. Amen.

Muscat Mission House.

"But I have received a number of letters from my friends and certain of the sheikhs and ulema in Beirut, begging me to return to them, pledging to find for me an honorable and lucrative position. I wrote them a reply full of gratitude for their zeal and kindness and their interest in my worldly prosperity; but informed them that God had given me sufficient support for this world, and for the world to come a better portion. I told them it was not God's will that I should return to Beirut at present, nor perhaps in the future, but that I shall die a stranger in a strange land through the love of God and of his Christ.

"After this my correspondence with them ceased. I long for letters from you. The Lord grant me patience and firm continuance in his love even unto death. Amen.

"As I have begun to write the history of my life from the beginning until now, I ask you to send me the date of my reception into the Evangelical Church. You can ascertain this from my first letter to Dr. Van Dyck, which he indorsed and sent to you. Please also give me the date of my going to Lebanon to school and especially the date of my baptism. Also send me the journal of my journey to el Makullah with our brother Mr. Zwemer, as well as my correspondence with my revered father. For all this I shall be very greatly obliged to you. Salute for me all your family, Dr. Van Dyck, Mr. Hardin and Rev. Yusef Bedr, and all who ask after me.

"Mr. Cantine and Mr. Sutton, of Kurachee, send their regards to you.

"Will you kindly send me a reply to these questions:

"I. Why is Jesus styled 'Aiesa' in the Moslem books? and did this name exist among the Arabs before Mohammed's time, during the 'Jahiliyeh,' or times of ignorance?

MUSCAT VIEWED FROM THE MISSION HOUSE.

"II. If drunkards can not enter the kingdom of God (1 Cor. 6 : 10) did not the Saviour, when changing the water into wine at the wedding in Cana, expose the guests to the peril of drunkenness, and thus of exclusion from the kingdom of God?

"III. Were the 'husks' of the parable of the Prodigal Son identical with the carob-pods of the kharrub-tree of Syria?

"IV. Is there any vital difference between the Arabic version of the Bible made by the Americans and that made by the Jesuits?

"Your obedient son in Christ,
"KAMIL ABDUL MESSIAH."

In response to this letter I mailed to him the letters and documents. His four questions indicate an active and studious mind, and my replies were in substance as follows:

"I. The name 'Aiesa' or 'Isa' is said by Baizawi to be the same as the Hebrew 'Ishua' and derived from Al-Ayas, 'white mingled with red.' The Arabic lexicons say that it is an Arabic or Syriac word, which may have been formed by inverting the order of the letters of 'Yesua,' which is also Hebrew, and thus think it is a corruption of Esau.

"II. Our Lord's miracle at Cana in no way encouraged drunkenness. At an oriental village wedding hundreds of people come together. Wine is given in very small cups or glasses. Sometimes all the population of the village and the neighboring villages assemble. To supply each one with a cupful of wine as large as half an eggshell would require a large quantity. Jesus saw that the supply was not large enough for the crowd assembled. The family were embarrassed, and exposed to severe reproach for failing in the duties of hospitality. He, therefore, turned the water into wine. There is no evidence that any one became intoxicated, nor is intoxication common at oriental weddings now, unless it be where European customs have come in and the poisonous arak and cognac are used.

"III. The husks of the parable are the same as the carob- or locust-pods of modern Syria.

"IV. The Jesuit translation of the Bible into Arabic differs very little from that of Drs. Eli Smith and Van Dyck, the points of difference being those of the Vulgate and the Textus Receptus of the Hebrew and Greek originals."

In the letter of June 19, 1891, Kamil asks about Mr. Van Tassell, a young American missionary who came to Syria to labor among the desert tribes. For purely political reasons, the Ottoman authorities objected to his going among the Arabs, and virtually expelled him from the frontier. Finding that he could not reach the desert tribes, for whom alone he was sent, he sold out his tents and camp equipage and returned to the United States. Dr. Ford purchased the waterproof tent, and it has been his summer home for five years. For the present the way of the gospel to the Bedawin

RESCUED SLAVE BOYS IN MUSCAT MISSION.

Arabs from the Syrian frontier is closed as thoroughly as the local governors can close it. It seems impossible for the official class to believe that a missionary like Mr. Van Tassell can have a purely spiritual and disinterested object. They suspect every "father of a hat" to be a secret political emissary of some European government. In some way, if it is not in our way, and at some time, if not in our time, the Lord will open the door of the gospel to the millions of the children of Ishmael.

Kamil's next letter is from Busrah, March 4, 1892, and indicates no little apprehension on his part of personal danger from fanatical Mohammedans.

After acknowledging the receipt of my letter and his great joy at the recovery of Mrs. Jessup from illness, he states that he had decided not to continue correspondence with his father, and asks affectionately about his friend, the converted Bedawi. He also asks for a copy of the " Bakurah " as soon as it is published, and intimates that, should the enemies of the gospel interfere with his work, he would return to Aden and labor with Mr. Gardner. He then says:

"In any case I will not go contrary to your counsels, for I am your obedient son in Christ. If you bid me go to death itself I shall not hesitate, and this your heart knows, for I am faithful to your bidding as long as I live. The Lord guide you to what is best for me and my people and preserve you and guide you with his eye, for the sake of the Lord Jesus Christ. Amen.

"Please salute most affectionately my honored friends Dr. Van Dyck and Mr. Hardin, and all the brethren, especially your own family.

"We have just learned of the sailing of a physician from our society to come to Busrah. The Lord bring him in safety.

"Your obedient son in Christ,

"KAMIL ABDUL MESSIAH."

KAMIL'S LAST LETTER.

The last letter in my possession from this beloved brother is dated April 22, 1892. He acknowledges gratefully the receipt of the documents previously asked for.

He says: "I am trying to act in accordance with your advice on the Lord's injunction, 'Be ye wise as serpents and harmless as doves,' and am careful about my spiritual work, as the Holy Spirit teaches me.

"Mr. Zwemer is anxious that I go boldly into the Moslem coffeehouses and streets now, during Ramadan, and preach Christ boldly. But I can see clearly that such a course would now be unwise and might drive us all out of el Busrah.

There is no religious liberty here as in Aden. A new helper has come here from Bagdad and the American doctor has come, but, not having visited Constantinople to get his diploma indorsed, he is helpless and must now go there for this purpose. I am writing a weekly report of my religious labors, which you will no doubt receive; so I will not copy it, as my time is fully occupied.

"Salute Dr. Van Dyck, who bade me, when I parted from him, 'Kamil, be wise as a fisherman in your work.' Would that I had the wise eye of the fisherman and the wisdom of the serpent.

"Salute also Mr. Hardin, and all inquiring friends.

"Your obedient son,
"KAMIL ABDUL MESSIAH."

Kamil's Journals in el Busrah.

The following extracts will show the zeal and fidelity with which he labored in season and out of season:

"April 1, 1892. As I was seated in the Kahweh (coffeehouse) and by my side —— Effendi and another man, the former asked me, 'What is the meaning of the "three persons in one God"? and what do you Christians believe about it?' I explained that we do not hold that there are three Gods, as the Koran claims; God forbid! We believe that there is one God who has no partner, and who is in three persons. The effendi replied, 'This is a strange doctrine, and your believing it is even stranger, as it can not enter the mind.' I replied, 'We can not refuse to believe everything that does not enter our minds. We must believe what God commands, whether it is within our comprehension or not. Our only course is to accept what God enjoins. There are many things as strange as the Trinity which men of all religions accept, as the eternity of God and his omnipresence, etc.; as we believe this, we must believe that, as God has thus revealed himself.'

"The same day three Sunnite Moslems and two shiahs called, and one Christian.

"On April 2d I invited a Turkish military officer to visit me. He asked a number of questions, and at length he began to curse the pope and his teachings contrary to the Bible, and to praise the Protestants in Bagdad. He loves the New Testament and asked me for a French Testament, which I gave him, and he went away grateful. During the day six Mohammedans and one Jew called on me.

"On the third day I was taken with violent fever, which continued until the seventh. On the eighth I went into el Busrah to visit my friends Saloma and Eliya. Then I returned and was invited by a friend to his house, where a large number of government officials were assembled, who were scribes and Pharisees. They plied me with questions such as how God could have a Son and how could the pope be infallible, etc. They accepted my declaration that the pope is not infallible; but as to Christ's being the Son of God they met the words with cursing and abuse on every side. My friend, the owner of the house, rose upon them and stopped their abuse. As I went out I shook the dust from my feet as Christ commanded me.

"April 13th. To-day I was accosted in the street by a Moslem to whom I gave a Bible about two months ago. He said, 'I read that book daily with my hareem and children, and this man, my cousin (sitting by him), would like a copy to read in his house.' I hastened and brought him the book, which he received gratefully, saying, 'We shall come and see you soon.' I replied, 'Ahlan wa sahlan,' *i. e.*, 'Welcome to you.'

"April 14th. A Persian Moslem, a Shiite, the Moolah Hassan, invited me to a place filled with Shiites, whose chief was the sayyid Nazir ed Din. Their object was to convince me of the truth of Islam, as they had heard that I am familiar with the Koran. When I entered the sayyid ordered me to be seated, and said, 'My dear son, we have heard that you know the Koran and the religion of Islam, and, fearful for the perdition of your soul, we have invited you here to enter the true religion.' He then asked, 'What do you think of the Koran? Is it true or not?' I replied, 'The Koran is the most elegant and rhetorical book in the Arabic language, as there are great books in other languages, as the French and English and others.' 'But,' he said, 'I ask you is it God's book or not?' 'This is a very important question,' I replied. 'If I say it is of God, you will say, "Why do you not believe it?" and if I say it is not, you will curse me; and you know that I am not a Moslem and do not believe it.' They then asked other questions and I answered them. At last they said, 'There is no profit in you; go to hell.' I said, 'God knows which of us will go to Jenneh and which to Jehennam.' They then said, 'Go and study the Koran.' I returned to my house, thanking God that I had escaped from them. Four Moslems came to call.

"April 15th. A Moslem effendi came and asked me for a Turkish Gospel, which I presented to him. Seven Moslems and a Christian called on me.

"April 19th To-day I visited a high military officer; a number of my friends were present.

He soon asked about my teaching and my pupils. I told him that I am teaching three Americans, one a doctor and two clergymen; but the doctor had been forbidden by the waly to practice, as his diploma is not visaed by the Constantinople Medical Board. He replied,

MUSCAT WOMEN COMING FROM MARKET.

'This waly does not know the difference between good and evil. Had he any brains he would not have prohibited a man from doing good.' One of those present remarked, 'The only object of these Americans is not doing good, but converting Moslems to the Protestant religion.' The officer said, 'The Protestant religion is Christianity, and these men force no one to accept their faith. If any one wants to come, they say, "Ahlan wa sahlan—welcome"; and to those who object they offer argument and proof. If any of you wish to discuss the matter, here is Kamil. Open the debate. If he convinces you, become Christians. If you convince him, he will become a Moslem.' I said, 'Agreed; I am ready if they are.' They replied 'Let the matter go now until another time.'

"During the day three Moslems and a Jew came to discuss with me.

"April 22d. As I was passing through the Kahweh at evening a company of my Moslem friends accepted my invitation and came to my house with a 'faqih' [a Mohammedan lawyer: the term is still retained in Spanish as alfaqui. Hughes' "Dict. of Islam"]. The discussion was as to whether Islam is a true religion, and their difficulties about the Trinity. They asked and I answered, and then I asked and they replied. Finally, on rising to take leave, they all prayed that Allah would enlighten my heart. And I also, after their departure, prayed to God to enlighten their minds and hearts that they might understand all they had heard.

"Five Moslems and two Christians called.

"April 23d. Four Roman Catholics called

and asked why we do not pray to Mary and reverence the pope and the priests and angels and others. I told them that I honored Mary more than they did; but as to the pope, I had no respect for him, on account of his arrogant conceit, but if he had the spirit and did the works of an apostle I would love him and honor him; and as to the priests, I would never ask one of them to forgive my sins, as they need to have their own sins forgiven. In all our talk the greatest indignation of these Romanists was at my not liking the pope.

"April 24th to 30th. I had conversation with thirty-seven Moslems, five Christians, and two Jews. On the 28th was 'Aieed el Futr' for both Sunnite and Shiah Moslems. I was unwell, and eleven Moslems and three Christians and one Jew came to see me. The next day I called upon eleven Mohammedan houses and we had discussions in three of them."

[Aieed el Futr is the great Moslem feast at the close of the Ramadan month of fasting, when all the Mohammedans spend three days in visiting and feasting. It is a time of rejoicing, when young and old in new and bright-colored clothing give themselves up to festivity. It answers to the Christian Easter Monday or the American Fourth of July.]

"During the week ending May 22d I had visits from twenty-three Moslems, five Christians, and one Jew, and sold two Bibles.

"May 22d to 28th. This week thirteen Moslems and five Christians called on me. On the 28th I went at 12 o'clock with my brother, Mr. Zwemer, to Majil. On our arrival the whole population, great and small, gathered around us, welcoming Mr. Zwemer and asking after his health with the greatest kindness and with smiling faces, as they had known him before. We then went with the crowd to the shade of a tree, where the multitude sat thirsting to hear the word of God. Mr. Zwemer then began to speak with great boldness on God's love to mankind, ending with that great verse which speaks of the greatness of God's love: 'God so loved the world, that he gave his only begotten Son, that whosoever believeth in him should not perish, but have everlasting life.' They made some objections and asked some questions, all of which he answered with love and gentleness and courtesy. I helped in answering some of the questions and they listened with eager interest. We then read several chapters from the Bible, from which also one of the boys read to them;

and as we had several copies of the Scriptures we gave them to those who could read, and they began to read, so that the company soon became like a great Sunday-school or church of forty or fifty members. As they read, Mr. Zwemer would ask them, 'Is this true? Is this

MOUNTAIN PASS IN OMAN.

true?' And do you suppose that they said 'No'? Not at all, but 'Yes, this is true.' Mr. Zwemer then explained in clear and simple language that we all are sinners in the sight of God, and that 'without shedding of blood there is no remission.' He then told them that the blood of Christ, shed on the 'wood of the cross,' is the only means to atone for our sin.

"It was a happy time to us, and the Spirit of God helped us mightily. At last Mr. Zwemer asked them, 'Is what you have heard true?' They said, 'Some things are true, and other things are true but we do not believe them.' He replied, 'Think over all you have heard.'

"At evening we bade them farewell and they accompanied us to the water, and we came home with great joy, crying unto God that he would cause his word to grow there and bring forth fruit meet for repentance."

Mr. Zwemer, in speaking of this visit, says, "For fully three and a half hours Kamil argued and reasoned with them from the Scriptures. We had prayer with the Moslems before we left."

Kamil's Death.

The sudden death of this gifted and godly young disciple was one of those bitter trials which can only be relieved by reference to the unerring wisdom of God, who doeth all things well.

It is the opinion of those associated with him that he was poisoned, but the hostility of the government, the fact that he was buried in the Moslem cemetery, and that no postmortem would have been allowed make it impossible to obtain positive proof.

The sad facts are as follows:

On Friday, June 24, 1892, Kamil died. Early in the morning Mr. Zwemer was called to conduct the funeral of the carpenter on board a foreign steamer. Owing to the extreme heat he did not call on Kamil before going home to breakfast. Mr. Cantine called on Kamil in the morning and found him suffering with symptoms of bowel disorder, violent vomiting and purging. Dr. Riggs, who was himself sick, sent him medicine by a servant. The heat was intense, and many of the people were prostrated with fevers. Kamil lived near the harbor, and the missionaries nearly two miles distant in the native quarter. At five o'clock P. M. Mr. Zwemer went to call on him and help him. Yakoob Yohanna, a Christian native, met him half way and told him of Kamil's death. He hastened to the house, and found it occupied by Turkish soldiers, mullahs, and people who had seized his papers, sealed up his room, and were busy with Moslem prayers over his body. They protested that he was a Moslem. Mr. Zwemer insisted that he was a Christian, and begged and entreated that he should be buried with Christian burial. The evidence of his

REV. S. M. ZWEMER AND MRS. ZWEMER—BAHREIN.

Christian faith was among the papers they had seized. But it was vain to resist this very exceptional display of armed force.

Mr. Zwemer left the body and went to the Turkish waly, and to appeal to the British consul. Meantime Mr. Cantine arrived, and

Mr. Zwemer had to hasten away on receipt of a note stating that Dr. Riggs was very ill, and with high temperature.

At 10.30 P. M. Mr. Cantine came with the news that the Moslems, in spite of his protest, had performed their funeral rites and buried Kamil. But the seal of the British consul was added to that of the Turks on the room containing his property. The next day the whole town was talking over the event. Many of the Moslems told the missionaries that they knew Kamil to be a Christian and a man of pure and upright life, that he was converted from Islam, and a preacher of Christianity.

The exact spot where the Moslems buried him could never be found. The consulate did not succeed in securing his little property, but his books and papers were afterwards sold at auction, excepting the few claimed by the missionaries as their personal property.

The evidence of foul play in his death is regarded as very strong :

I. He was a young man of strong physique and had not been long unwell.

II. Had he died from ordinary disease none

but his companions would have known it, and the missionaries would have been told of it before any one else.

III. It is regarded as impossible that the Turks and mullahs could have prepared his body for burial, sealed all his property, and had the military police agree to oppose any help or interference on the part of the missionaries, in so short a time as that which intervened between his death and their arrival. The washing and enshrouding of the body according to Moslem custom is a long and elaborate ceremony, and the sheikhs and mullahs must repeat the "Kalimet esh Shehadad," or word of witness, "There is no deity but Allah, and Mohammed is his apostle," at every ablution, and three times after the washing, when three pots of camphor and water are poured over the body.

The following are two of the prayers recited by Moslems at a funeral :

> "God is Great.
> Holiness to thee, oh God,
> And to thee be praise.
> Great is thy Name.
> Great is thy greatness.
> Great is thy praise.
> There is no deity but thee."

"O God, forgive our living and our dead, and those of us who are present and those who are absent, and our children and our full-grown persons, our men and our women. O God, those whom thou dost keep alive amongst us keep alive in Islam, and those whom thou causest to die let them die in the faith."

Those who place the corpse in the grave repeat the following sentence:

"We commit thee to earth in the name of God and in the religion of the prophet."

IV. Government officials were on hand to take possession of all his effects and seal up his room before his Christian brethren could arrive.

There is every indication that poison had been given him by some unknown persons, either in coffee, the usual eastern way of giving it, or as medicine.

V. The burial took place in the evening and the place of interment was concealed.

VI. According to the Moslem law, "a male apostate (murtadd) is liable to be put to death, if he continue obstinate in his error. If a boy under age apostatize, he is not to be put to death, but to be imprisoned until he come to full age, when, if he continue in the state of unbelief, he must be put to death." According to Dr. Hughes, quoting from the book "Sahih ul Bukhari," "Ikrimah relates that some apostates were brought to the Khalifa Ali, and he burnt them alive; but Ibn Abbas heard of it and said that the Khalifa had not acted rightly, for the prophets had said, " Punish not with God's punishment (*i. e.*, fire), but whosoever changes his religion, kill him with the sword."

VII. Kamil's own father once wrote him virtually threatening to kill him as an apostate.

In these days the sword is not generally used to dispose of apostates from the faith. Strychnine or corrosive sublimate are more convenient, and less apt to awaken public notice, especially where an autopsy would not be allowed.

It may be that Kamil's father used the language simply for intimidation, for I can hardly believe him to be so utterly devoid of natural affection; but religious fanaticism, whether originating in Arabia or in Rome, seems to override all laws of human affection or tenderness.

The Lord himself, the chief Shepherd, knows

whether his loving child Kamil is worthy of a martyr's crown. We know that he was faithful unto death. He fought the good fight, he kept the faith, he finished his course. His life has proved that the purest and most unsullied flowers of grace in character may grow even in the atmosphere of unchristian social life. It mattered not to him who buried him or where he was buried. He was safe beyond the reach of persecution and harm.

I have rarely met a more pure and thoroughly sincere character, *sinc cera*. From the beginning of our acquaintance in "our flowery bright Beirut," to his last days on the banks of the Tigris, he was a model of a humble, cheerful, courteous, Christian gentleman.

Kamil's history is a rebuke to our unbelief in God's willingness and power to lead Mohammedans into a hearty acceptance of Christ and his atoning sacrifice.

We are apt to be discouraged by the closely riveted and intense intellectual aversion of these millions of Moslems to the doctrines of the Trinity and of the divinity of Jesus Christ. But Kamil's intellectual difficulties about the Trinity vanished when he felt the need of a divine Saviour. He seemed taught by the Spirit of God from the first. He exclaimed frequently at the wonderful scheme of redemption through the atoning work of Christ.

"El fida, el fida," "redemption" he once said to me, "redemption, how wonderful! I now see how God can be just and justify the sinner. We have nothing of this in Islam. We talk of God's mercy, but we can not see how his justice is to be satisfied." What the Mohammedan needs above all things is a sense of sin, of personal sin, and of his need of a Saviour.

According to Islam, a man obtains salvation by a recital of the "Kalimah" or creed, but if he be an evil-doer he will suffer the pains of a purgatorial fire until his sins are atoned for.

The two words in the Koran which express the doctrine of expiation are, first, "Kaffarah," (Sura 5 : 49): "And therein (Ex. 21 : 23) have we enacted for them 'Life for life, an eye for eye and nose for nose and ear for ear and tooth for tooth, and for wounds retaliation'; whoso shall compromise it as alms shall have therein the expiation of his sin." "The expiation of a mistaken word in your oaths shall be to feed ten poor persons," etc. (Sura 5:91). And, second, "Fidyah" (Sura 2:180): "Those who are fit to fast and do not, the expiation of this shall be the maintenance of a poor man." Whosoever is sick and can not make the pilgrimage to Mecca "must expiate by fasting or alms or an offering." In Moslem theology the term "kaffaratu'z zunub," "the atonement for sins," is used for the duties of prayer, fasting, almsgiving, and pilgrimage. The visiting of shrines of the saints is also an atonement for sins. "Ziyaratu-'l-kubur" is "kaffaratu-z-zunub." In all these cases expiation is man's act, one of the meritorious acts of a religion of works.

Sacrifices are common among Moslems on the great feast of "El Azha", and on the birth of a child, "Aquiqah." But in none of these is there any expiatory character. Mohammedanism ignores the doctrine that "without shedding of blood is no remission." (Lev. 17:11; Heb. 9:22.) It knows no offering for sin. Its numerous formal prayers, its fast, pilgrimage, and almsgiving, satisfy the conscience with the idea of the efficacy of human merit.

But a sense of personal demerit, a conviction of sin before a just and holy God, reveals the emptiness of these outward works, and drives the sinner to seek a Saviour. Kamil felt this deeply and expressed it in his prayers and his conversation. Arguments on the divinity of Christ will avail little with a man who does not feel the need of a divine redeemer. And when he feels this need he does not need the arguments. "An incarnation in order to redemption" is the foundation of Christian theology. If we feel our need of a redeemer, we can not be satisfied with any less person than God incarnate. Let us remember this in laboring for Mohammedans. They need to feel the enormity of sin against a just and holy God. They need no new gospel, but the old, old story, told in the old, old way.

In May, 1868, I visited Williams' book store, in Boston, in company with that noble Christian lady, Mrs. Walter Baker. On entering, she introduced me to her old friend, Oliver Wendell Holmes, as "a missionary to Syria." He was most affable and cordial, and asked me about the country and people, and at length said, "How do you preach to those Mohammedans? do you teach the orthodox theology?" I replied, "We preach to them the same gospel that we would preach to any other poor sinners—that man is a sinner against a just and holy God and needs a divine Saviour. They need the same salvation that we do." He then stepped to the book shelves, and taking down a copy of his work, "Elsie Venner," presented it to me, saying, "This is my theology." I turned to the counter, and taking up a Bible, replied, "And this is my theology." "What!" said he, "do you mean to say that you accept that whole Bible, from Genesis to Revelation, and believe it all?" "Certainly," said I, "with all my heart." He stepped back and surveyed me intently from head to foot, and then said, with a smile to Mrs. Baker, "Well, it is refreshing to see a man who believes something."

And it is refreshing to have such a Bible and such a gospel to believe. It meets our highest and our deepest wants, the exacting cravings of our nature. We must have a Saviour, and we can not rest in any one short of a divine Saviour, the incarnate Son of God.

APPENDIX.

THE ARABIAN MISSION.

This mission, with which Kamil was connected until the day of his death, originated in the New Brunswick Theological Seminary of the Reformed Church in America. It was organized in 1889 on an undenominational basis, because the Foreign Board did not feel equal to the responsibility of the care of the mission in addition to the growing needs of their other mission fields. In 1894, however, the mission was adopted by the Reformed Church, although retaining its separate financial status.

This is not the place to give the brief history of the progress of this mission in the face of many obstacles and difficulties both at home and abroad, but a short statement of the present condition and work of the mission in the field will show what God hath wrought.

The mission at present occupies eastern Arabia on the coast with three stations and two out-stations. Busrah vilayet on the north has an area of fifty thousand square miles, about the size of New York State, and a population of seven hundred thousand. The Bahrein islands with the adjacent coast have a population of about three hundred thousand, and Oman, with Muscat as chief city, five hundred thousand. Work was begun at Busrah in 1891, Bahrein, 1892, Muscat, 1893. Amara, on the Tigris, north of Busrah, was occupied as an outstation in 1895 and this year work was auspiciously begun at Nasariyeh on the Euphrates, near the site of Ur of the Chaldees.

When a large building is not yet in process of construction, and the foundations only are being laid, the plan of the architect can best be seen from the model, and not amid the diggings and stone-breaking and loose material. How much more is this true when the great Architect is laying the foundations for his spiritual temple in eastern Arabia? When two of us came to the peninsula five years ago we were permitted to stretch the measuring line from corner to corner, and on our knees study God's plan for the building. Since then we have received, once and again, reinforcements, but even now the foundations are only beginning to be laid, and there is so much rubbish about that it is hard to see much progress from year to year in the superstructure. While other missions can speak of harvest time, and give statistics of churches, schools, and baptisms, we are yet in the midst of early sowing, and the statistics we can give all refer to the seedtime of the spoken and printed word.

From each station as a center, and from the northernmost limit of the Busrah vilayet, for more than a thousand miles along the coast of Arabia to Ras el-Had, our colporteurs offer God's word to all who will receive it, and speak with all who will hear. They are the real pioneer evangelists, and their work breaks down prejudice and opens the way for work of all kinds in the future. Six colporteurs were employed for a whole or part of the year, and the five bookshops were open for twelve months without intermission. At Busrah a small circulating library for English-reading natives was started in connection with the Bible Depot, and the stock of Arabic and English educational books is growing larger. Our prime object is, of course, the circulation of the Scriptures. To this end our mission receives aid from the American Bible Society for Bahrein and Muscat, and from the British and Foreign Bible Society for Busrah and Amara; and it has only been from lack of missionaries to accompany the colporteurs, and so extend their journeys into new territory, that the annual circulation has not still more increased. As it is, the number of portions of the Bible sold this year is five hundred more than last year. Of these sales eighty-seven per cent. were made to Moslems.

The religious books include the recent controversial Arabic and Persian literature, the standard Christian classics and many by Spurgeon, Moody, and others from the Beirut press. Our educational books are often the bait on the hook of the shopkeeper in fishing for men, and yet more often even a geography or primer will so break through prejudice that the Moslem lad who has bought and read either, comes again and again to the Christian bookshop. In all our shops the walls themselves witness to Christ the Son of God, and no one can enter them and remain ignorant of our message.

It is especially encouraging to note that the sale of complete Bibles and Testaments is on the increase where earlier sales of smaller portions have prepared the way. The following table shows the totals and increase of Scripture sales for five years in eastern Arabia:

TOTAL SALES SCRIPTURES—ARABIAN MISSION.

1893	1894	1895	1896
825	1760	2313	2805

Almost identified with our Bible work is that

of preaching the gospel in regions beyond our three stations by journeys on sea and land. From Busrah, north and south, the rivers are the great, cheap, and safe highways of travel. The long journey up the Tigris to Koot, across the plain of the Shatt el Hai, at Nasariyeh, is made twice a year. Between our three stations steamers ply the gulf and we try to make each journey a missionary tour. The importance of itineration in a pioneer field can not easily be exaggerated. Even as Kamil preached the word on the south coast, his successors, our colporteurs, recently visited the eastern pirate coast south of Bahrein and left behind them a hundred and one books among Arabs who formerly made the whole coast unsafe, but have now settled down to fishing and commerce. In Oman the Rev. P. J. Zwemer has penetrated far into the interior and found the whole mountain region fertile, populous, and accessible. The people, too, were agricultural and not nomadic, and many of them could read. On two occasions the highlands of Yemen were visited, and evangelistic work was attempted among the large Jewish population of Sanaa. Kateef and Hassa with its old capital, Hofhoof, also heard for the first time the word of life from missionary lips.

From the outset medical mission work has

proved a very efficient adjunct to our work of evangelization. Dr. Riggs left the mission field shortly after Kamil's death, and his successor failed in health. But our present medical missionary, Dr. H. R. L. Worrall, has regained lost ground and the work is growing. The dispensary at Busrah is a daily pulpit where we enjoy every freedom to preach Christ. Here either a missionary or a colporteur reads the Scriptures and prays with the patients, tracts and leaflets are distributed, and the spirit of the gospel is acted out before the eyes of the dullest Arab in a way that can not be misunderstood. Last year the total number of cases was 4345.

By ministering to their bodies at the dispensaries in Busrah and Bahrein, by visiting villages and huts, by reading the gospel, by teaching morals, Mrs. Zwemer has inaugurated a hopeful work for our Arabian sisters. Nowhere and at no time since coming to our mission was she subjected to any annoyance or rudeness from the Arabs, although many had never before seen a white woman. And it has been abundantly demonstrated through her journeys and experiences that the door for such work is widely open and may prove of untold blessing if others, like minded, come out to join her in the work for Arabia.

In the earliest printed plan of the Arabian mission there was reference to work for slaves, and because Oman is the home of the African slave-dealer, Mackay, of Uganda, pleaded for an Arab mission. It was only another link in the plan of God's providence, therefore, that on May 27, 1896, Mr. P. J. Zwemer felt called to receive and care for eighteen rescued slaves in addition to his other work at Muscat. Although the experiment is not yet completed, the results so far are most gratifying, and the boys are making excellent progress in morals and education. Immediately after they came they were put into manual training, making baskets, sewing, and housework. Being ignorant of any language but Swaheli, it was thought best that they be taught English first. After primary instruction by means of charts, they showed enough mental capacity to warrant the expense of a teacher; and S. M. David, an Indian Christian, formerly a teacher in the C. M. S. Freed-Slave School at Nasik, India, came to Muscat on September 15th. All the boys have since made such rapid progress in the three Rs that they are almost prepared for the first Indian standard. The health of all the lads has been good with one exception, and they are apparently perfectly at home in the Muscat climate. Instruction is given them from the Bible and by means of a simple catechism; their moral sense is growing, and many of them begin to realize the opportunity of the new life open before them. The boys are also learning to assist in printing with a small hand press Christian literature for the Arabs. It is the day of small things, but the first Arabic leaflet sent from this press has already made a stir among the dead bones and awakened thought as well as hostility.

Such is a brief sketch of the present work of the Arabian mission and its methods. Further information can be obtained from its secretary, Rev. H. N. Cobb, D. D., 25 E. 22d Street, New York City. Arabia pleads loudly for more missionaries. The country is accessible nearly everywhere, and the people are willing to hear the word. Only a small part of the peninsula is under Turkish rule, and more and more God's providence is calling to the great task of evangelizing the Mohammedan world. May the story of Kamil's life stir many to a like consecration and devotion for the honor of our Saviour and to bring back to the fold of Christ the lost sheep of the house of Ishmael.

S. M. ZWEMER.

www.ingramcontent.com/pod-product-compliance
Lightning Source LLC
Chambersburg PA
CBHW030335170426
43202CB00010B/1138